Vintage BROWNS

Also by Terry Pluto

ON SPORTS:

Vintage Cavs
The Browns Blues
The Comeback: LeBron, the Cavs and Cleveland
Glory Days in Tribe Town (with Tom Hamilton)
Joe Tait: It's Been a Real Ball (with Joe Tait)
Things I've Learned from Watching the Browns
LeBron James: The Making of an MVP (with Brian Windhorst)
The Franchise (with Brian Windhorst)
Dealing: The Cleveland Indians' New Ballgame
False Start: How the New Browns Were Set Up to Fail
The View from Pluto
Unguarded (with Lenny Wilkens)
Our Tribe
Browns Town 1964
Burying the Curse
The Curse of Rocky Colavito
Falling from Grace
Tall Tales
Loose Balls
Bull Session (with Johnny Kerr)
Tark (with Jerry Tarkanian)
Forty-Eight Minutes, a Night in the Life of the NBA (with Bob Ryan)
Sixty-One (with Tony Kubek)
You Could Argue But You'd Be Wrong (with Pete Franklin)
Weaver on Strategy (with Earl Weaver)
The Earl of Baltimore
Super Joe (with Joe Charboneau and Burt Graeff)
The Greatest Summer

ON FAITH AND OTHER TOPICS:

Faith and You
Faith and You, Volume 2
Everyday Faith
Champions for Life: The Power of a Father's Blessing (with Bill Glass)
Crime: Our Second Vietnam (with Bill Glass)

Vintage BROWNS

A Warm Look Back at the CLEVELAND BROWNS of the 1970s, '80s, '90s and More

TERRY PLUTO

GRAY & COMPANY, PUBLISHERS
CLEVELAND

Gray & Company, Publishers
www.grayco.com

ISBN 978-1-59851-119-2
Printed in the United States of America
1.1a

To Mike Jozic, a wonderful "son"
and a Vintage Browns fan.

CONTENTS

Vintage BROWNS

Vintage Browns fans at Municipal Stadium on Jan. 4, 1981.
C.H. Pete Copeland / The Plain Dealer

WHY THIS BOOK? WHY NOW?

I have written four books on the Cleveland Browns. Thinking back, all of them have been inspired by some type of pain.

That's right, pain.

That even includes "Browns Town 1964," the story of the Browns' championship season. It's an upbeat account of a very likable team that pulled off one of the biggest upsets in NFL title game history—a 27-0 victory over the heavily favored Baltimore Colts.

The book was written in 1996 and 1997, not long after the Browns moved to Baltimore. That's one of those "Only In Cleveland" sports stories. The last time the Browns won an NFL title, they beat the team from Baltimore. Then Baltimore lost the Colts to Indianapolis in 1984. A decade later, still looking for a team, the city of Baltimore schemed with Browns owner Art Modell to hijack the Browns.

So the team that beat Baltimore then moved to Baltimore . . . to replace the franchise Baltimore had lost.

I wrote "Browns Town 1964" to capture the feeling when Cleveland was Browns Town. I had an idea the NFL would eventually return to Cleveland, but as what? An expansion team? A stolen team from another city?

That led to my second Browns book: "False Start."

Oh boy . . .

The Browns were back in Cleveland in 1999, but under the worst conditions the NFL had ever granted an expansion franchise. "False Start" was the story of how everyone from Art Modell to Baltimore to the NFL stuck it to Browns fans.

Then, talk about doubling down on the pain . . . the old Browns now in Baltimore won the 2001 Super Bowl.

Sigh.

My third Browns book was "Things I Learned From Watching The Browns."

That came out in 2010, a decade after the Browns returned. It was an informal history of the Browns. I touched on The Fumble, The Drive, The Move and why Art Modell doesn't belong in the Hall of Fame but Clay Matthews does. There also was a chapter about why a man named Brown should have the first statue in front of FirstEnergy Stadium.

That was Paul Brown, the father of the Browns and the man Bill Belichick considers the greatest coach in the history of pro football. Belichick delivered that opinion to me as we exchanged emails. I wanted to interview Belichick for that book about his years in Cleveland, including 1995 when the team moved.

He rejected that request with two words: "Too painful."

I know that Browns fans revel in their football heartbreak. But at least the teams of the 1980s with Red Right 88, The Drive, etc., were good enough to make you care.

By 2017, the Browns had become the worst franchise in the NFL (in terms of wins and losses) since returning in 1999.

Several readers asked me to do an updated version of "False Start." Why do things keep going wrong for their favorite team?

That led to "Browns Blues," published in 2018. The title indeed says it all. No football fan base can sing the blues quite like Browns fans.

Pain . . . PAIN . . . PAIN!

And yes, even MORE PAIN!!!

But not this time. Not this book.

This book was inspired by a series of stories I wrote for The Plain Dealer. They detailed the memories of former Browns players about the day they were drafted. It didn't take long for the players from the 1970s and 1980s to dominate my reporting.

Look at the names: Bernie Kosar, Doug Dieken, Reggie Langhorne, Kevin Mack, Earnest Byner, Brian Brennan, Greg Pruitt and Ozzie Newsome. This book has even more.

Then it hit me: These are Vintage Browns for people of a certain age—middle age.

This book also has profiles of four players from the "new Browns," post-1999.

Why them?

I like them as people. I respect them as players.

For all of these players, enough time has passed to give fans a sense of heartfelt gratitude rather than heartbreak when it comes to memories of those teams.

I also became fascinated with the Bill Belichick tenure in Cleveland. Did he give many hints of the greatness to follow after he became the coach of the New England Patriots? The Belichick Era in Cleveland was generally one of frustration and anger, with the exception of the 1994 playoff season. It ended when Modell moved the team to Baltimore after the 1995 season—and fired Belichick.

But after the angst and agony, there was forgiveness. Kosar and Belichick have an appreciation of each other. Reggie Langhorne was tormented by Belichick during a contract negotiation. The NFL ruled Belichick unfairly fined Langhorne. But now these men are friends.

Kosar is a pivotal figure in this book. He opened his heart to me and to readers about the fears he felt when he first came to the Browns. The weight of the Browns and their fans were on his young shoulders. The hometown hero playing for his hometown team often has led to failure.

Not this time. Not Kosar.

Looking back now, what he and those late 1980s teams accomplished is even more impressive.

I also wrote about Marty Schottenheimer, the best Browns coach since Paul Brown/Blanton Collier in the 1950s-60s. Why did Schottenheimer really leave the Browns? I uncovered that strange story.

This book was so much fun to write. The former players were fascinating to interview. The stories had a special appeal to me because in the 1980s, I was covering the Tribe and then the Cavaliers. I rarely got to write about the Browns.

I became a sports columnist in 1993 for the Akron Beacon Journal. That's when I became a regular at Browns games. So I was like a lot of the younger fans. Most of what I saw from the Browns was dismal.

The book ends with two Browns from the "Browns Town 1964" era, because I couldn't resist adding two of my favorites. Ernie Green was one of the most underrated Browns ever. And defensive end Bill Glass was instrumental in growing my faith and becoming involved in prison ministry.

Revisiting vintage Browns is a great way to experience the joy of the guys and some of those terrific teams.

TAPE IT UP AND PLAY: DOUG DIEKEN

If you listen to Doug Dieken, you begin to think his entire career could be summed up with these words: "Better to be lucky than good."

The good-natured Dieken tends to make you think that belongs on his tombstone.

Lucky? Of course Dieken was blessed by fate at certain key points in his life. That's true of many successful people.

But that doesn't tell you much about Dieken. This self-effacing man has a relentless spirit. Part of his career is due to a willingness to show up consistently with a good attitude. And it's a willingness to adapt to change without much complaining.

Consider when Dieken was drafted by the Browns . . .

Those words might surprise some people who listen to Dieken broadcast Browns games on radio with Jim Donovan. Even some Browns players over the years had no idea Dieken wore an orange helmet for 14 years. Or that he still has the NFL record for consecutive starts by a left tackle—194.

Or that he still has a hard time figuring out how that happened.

"I wasn't even supposed to be a tackle," said Dieken. "I didn't even know I had that consecutive game record until a guy at Cleveland Clinic told me when I was there for my brother's heart surgery. The guy there looked me up on his phone and told me about it."

We'll get to that story and some others in a moment. But first, a few things to know.

The 72-year-old Dieken is an engaging storyteller, but also a good listener. He is a caring man with very little ego. He's been doing Browns games on the radio since 1985, missing only two. In many ways, Dieken has been like the national anthem for the Browns ever since opening day of the 1971 season—he's part of every game.

* * *

The year was 1971, long before the NFL draft was a media event.

"On draft day, I was sitting at home waiting for a team to call," said Dieken. "I was watching TV. Not the draft. It wasn't on back then. My mother was upstairs with her bridge club."

This was in Streator, Illinois, where Dieken grew up. The town of about 13,000 is about 90 miles southwest of Chicago.

"The phone rang. I picked it up," said Dieken.

"This is Nick Skorich, head coach of the Cleveland Browns," said the man on the line. "We just drafted you in the sixth round as an offensive tackle."

Dieken paused for a second, wondering if they had the right guy. He'd never played tackle at Illinois. He was the team's leading receiver for three years as a tight end.

"Any chance I could play tight end?" Dieken asked Skorich.

"We'll see when you get here," said the coach.

That was the end of the conversation.

Dieken went upstairs to tell his bridge-playing mother about being drafted by the Browns.

"That's nice," she said.

Then she looked back at the ladies and said, "Three clubs."

* * *

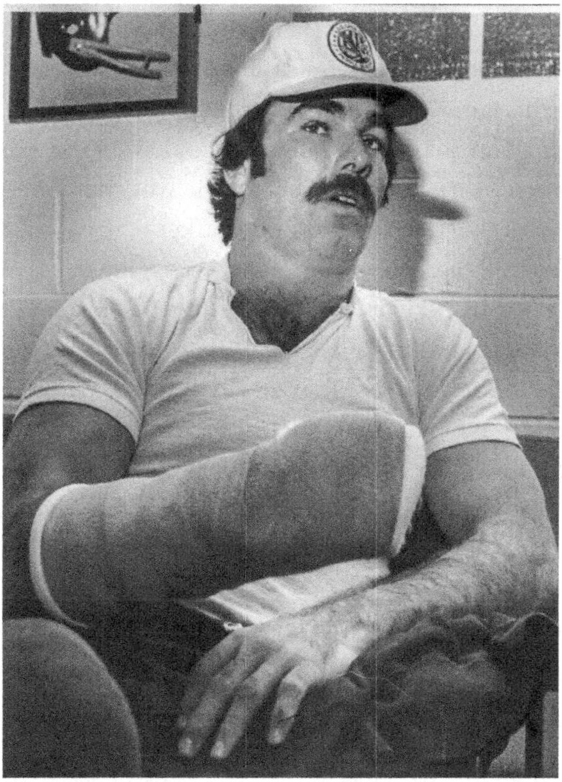

Doug Dieken with broken right hand in 1982. Playing despite injuries is one reason why he still has the NFL record for consecutive starts by a left tackle. He was also one of the best left tackles in the NFL during his era.
Richard T. Conway / Plain Dealer

Dieken was 6-foot-5 in high school, a star basketball player and baseball pitcher. His town was small, without much youth football. He didn't play the sport when he was young. Dieken had a brother who was 6-foot-8. He assumed he'd grow to be at least that tall, and basketball would be his ticket to college.

"The high school basketball coach said he wanted me to get in shape in the fall before basketball started," said Dieken. "He wanted me to run cross country or play football."

"That's an easy decision," Dieken told the coach. "Football." He wanted no part of running miles and miles in cross country.

While his family didn't own a farm, his father managed them.

"He gave me all the lousy jobs he could find like baling hay," said Dieken. "He wanted to see if I could work hard. My mother's family was in the grain commodity market."

Along with agriculture, Streator "was the glass container capital of the world back then," according to Dieken. His parents were graduates of the University of Illinois, so Dieken expected to go to college. This is Midwest small town. While the movie "Hoosiers" was set in rural Indiana, the landscape and the sense of place reflects where Dieken was raised.

When you head out of town, the fields are flat. The sunsets are gorgeous, as the reds and yellows burst across the big sky of the plains.

It was not a place where you grew up thinking about playing pro football. The NFL seemed to be a million galaxies away—even for a very good high school athlete.

And Dieken was indeed very good.

By his junior season, Dieken surprised himself by being an All-State wide receiver. In basketball, he led his team by averaging 12.6 points and 9.5 rebounds.

"But I shot about 35% from the foul line," said Dieken.

Actually, it was 47%.

In his final baseball game of his senior year, he threw a no-hitter.

"And I lost, 1-0," he said, laughing.

The accidental football player ended up being a two-time All-State selection. He was recruited by Big Ten schools and picked Illinois, the university his parents had attended.

* * *

When Dieken arrived at Illinois, he never saw what was coming.

"The basketball and football coaches were fired because of a scandal having to do with a slush fund," said Dieken. "The NCAA said I didn't have to honor my commitment. I could go anywhere, but I stayed. Jim Valek was the new coach, the poor guy. None of us knew how bad it would be."

Dieken's team had records of 1-9 and 0-10 in his first two seasons. Back then, freshmen didn't play varsity football. The team was 2-4 in Dieken's senior year and some boosters and members of the athletic department wanted to fire Valek.

"We were playing Ohio State," said Dieken. "I had heard they wanted to fire Coach (Valek) after the game. We lost (48-29). After the game, Woody Hayes said, 'That coach they want to fire—they ought to fire me, because that guy out-coached me.' "

After the game, the team was informed that Valek was being fired. Dieken asked all the coaches to leave the room.

"Hey guys," Dieken told his teammates. "If Coach isn't here on Monday, I'm not going to be here. Anybody want to go with me?"

The players raised their hands. The team sent a letter to the athletic department saying they either keep Valek or the players would refuse to play next week.

"They had an emergency meeting and rehired him for the rest of the season," said Dieken. "Back then, they didn't fire coaches in the middle of the season. It wasn't right."

Valek was rehired. The team finished 3-7.

This story says something about Dieken, who generally is a go-along, get-along guy. He has a sense of right-and-wrong. When something was flat-out wrong, the man from the Midwest was willing to stand up and say it—and challenge others to follow.

He did that when playing with the Browns, demanding better play and harder work from some of his fellow offensive lineman.

As Dieken talked about his college football days, he mentioned Tim McCarthy, a walk-on football player who was a soccer player. On March 31, 1981, President Ronald Reagan was shot. Dieken saw McCarthy's picture flashed on the television set.

"He was the Secret Service guy who took a bullet for the president," said Dieken. "He was one of about 30 of us in that first football class. I think there were only five left by the time we graduated."

* * *

After his draft-day conversation with Skorich in 1971, Dieken was still trying to figure out why they wanted him to play tackle. As far as he knew, only one NFL scout ever showed up at an Illinois practice.

"It was Lou Groza," said Dieken. "I never talked to him. We knew who he was (a former Browns player). But that was it."

Dieken played in the Blue-Gray all-star game and the Senior Bowl, two senior showcases. Dieken was a first-team All-Big Ten tight end, and was in that position in both postseason games. Future Browns coach Sam Rutigliano coached the receivers in the Senior Bowl.

Rutigliano must have had some influence on the play calling.

"They didn't throw a pass to a tight end all day, everything was to the receivers," laughed Dieken.

The Browns still picked him, the 142nd selection, in the 1971 draft.

"I showed up at the old Fleming Field at Case Western (Reserve University) for rookie camp," said Dieken. "They handed me jersey No. 73 and pointed me toward the offensive line."

The message was clear: 73 was a number for a lineman. (Years later it would be the number of Browns star left tackle Joe Thomas.)

* * *

Dieken's first contract had a $5,000 bonus. The salary was $16,000 (not guaranteed) with a chance to earn another $6,000 in incentives if he played more.

When he was measured, he remembered to stand as tall as possible. A scout at the Senior Bowl had told him that if he measured at least 6-foot-5, it could be worth an extra 500 bucks. He came in at 6-foot-5, 235 pounds.

He signed his contract. He spent the night at the old Hollenden House hotel in downtown Cleveland with the other rookies. The next day he met owner Art Modell and some coaches at Municipal Stadium. When it was over, a member of the front office was supposed to drive Dieken to the airport. Instead, he dropped Dieken off at the Terminal Tower.

"He told me to take the train going west," said Dieken. "When it ends, get off—that's the airport."

Not exactly a coddled rookie.

"I saw only one NFL game in my life before I got to the Browns," he said. "It actually was the Browns. They were playing the Bears at Wrigley Field."

Dieken has one distinct memory from that game.

"Dick Butkus was playing linebacker for the Bears," he said. "He hit (Browns running back) Ron Johnson and I thought he killed Johnson."

A few years later, Dieken met Johnson and mentioned the hit.

"I thought he killed you."

"So did I," said Johnson.

* * *

When Dieken joined the Browns, they put him at left tackle—behind veteran Dick Schafrath. Late in training camp, he was told to go see Skorich. The coach explained they were putting him on waivers with the idea of eventually having him on the "taxi squad," or practice squad as it's known today.

Dieken was confused. It sounded as if he was being cut. Then he received word he was claimed by Miami. It turned out one of Miami's assistant coaches was Monte Clark, a former Browns lineman. He called current Browns lineman Gene Hickerson, who praised Dieken.

The Browns scrambled, pulling back the waivers. He ended up making the team.

Why all the roster manipulation? The Browns were trying to keep third-round pick Paul Staroba on the team. Just imagine if the Browns had let Dieken go—to protect an all-Big Ten receiver from Michigan whose NFL career consisted of 10 games and two receptions.

But at this point, Dieken was a sixth-rounder learning a new position in the NFL. He was mostly on special teams early in his rookie season. Then right tackle Bob McKay became injured.

"I went in, and I'd never played right tackle in my life," said Dieken. "I played maybe three quarters at left tackle in the preseason games. No tackle in college."

Dieken survived. When McKay healed, Dieken returned to the bench. But a few games later, an angry Skorich benched veterans Jim Houston, Gary Collins and Schafrath. In his book, "Heart of a Mule," Schafrath said he learned of the changes in The Plain Dealer. He was in his 13th NFL season and his body was falling apart.

Dieken became the starting left tackle on Nov. 21, 1971. He stayed there until Dec. 16, 1984, never missing a start.

"The biggest adjustment was pass blocking," he said. "But then I figured out it was like blocking out your man in basketball. Instead of keeping your body between the man and the rim, it was keeping your body between the man and the quarterback. You square him up. Footwork is the key."

Then Dieken explained that one part of the way he played the position was wrong.

"If you play left tackle, your left hand is on the ground and your left leg is back," he said. "But I played with my right hand in the dirt, the right leg back. It was backwards."

Early in his career, no one bothered to change him. Later on, he played for Howard Mudd—considered one of the best offensive line coaches in NFL history.

"Why didn't you change me?" Dieken asked Mudd.

"You're playing it well," Mudd said. "No need."

* * *

When talking to Dieken, the conversation becomes like a winding country road with a few side trips. For example, Dieken explained he never used an agent when talking contract.

"It's almost like salaries were slotted back then," said Dieken. "You know what starting offensive linemen made, and that was about what you'd get."

Dieken played 14 seasons, doing all his own contracts. His highest salary was $250,000.

"If nothing else, I saved a lot in agent fees," he said.

Dieken said some of the guys on the team once asked him how he negotiated with Modell.

"It's easy," said Dieken.

He knelt down and said, "Please Art, please play me!"

Dieken laughed.

"That was my strategy—begging," he said.

* * *

Early in his career, Dieken's teammates would tell him, "We never should have traded Eppie Barney."

Who?

"Eppie Barney," said Dieken. "The Browns traded him to the Bears for the draft pick they used on me."

Eppie Barney was from Cleveland and had played at Collinwood High and Iowa State. He was a third-round pick by the Browns in 1967. The receiver played only 26 games in the NFL, catching 19 passes.

Dieken loves to tell this type of story, going for laughs at his own expense.

* * *

How do you play 194 games in a row at left tackle in the NFL? You don't just play hurt, you play injured. You play when you know you should sit. If you're Dieken, you play through the pain because you remember something your father said.

"What life gives you, you handle it," said Dieken. "Life gave me left tackle."

Dieken was not about to let it go. In the middle of his second season, something was wrong with his right knee. He went to see the team doctor.

"You need surgery," Dieken was told. "You tore a cartilage. You can have the operation and miss the rest of the season. Or you can tape it up and play."

He taped it up and played. Surgery after the season.

Then right before the opening game of his third season, something was wrong with his other knee.

"You tore the cartilage," he was told. "You can have surgery and miss the season, or you can tape it up and play."

Same story, different knee. He taped it up and played. Surgery after the season. There were three knee surgeries in his career. And broken hands. Broken thumbs. Torn tendons, strained ligaments. He played wearing a cast on a fractured arm.

"I had a concussion or two," he said. "Maybe four or six. Hard to know."

He played.

"That's what you did back then," said Dieken.

By the end of the 1984 season, he knew his body couldn't take it anymore. He retired. Since then, he's had both knees replaced. Both hips replaced. A degenerative disk in his back.

Dieken laughed. He knows the litany of injuries and all the pain is not funny, but what else can you do? But he did what he always did.

He played.

* * *

In 1984, Dieken knew his career was about over. Browns radio broadcaster Gib Shanley asked him what he planned to do next. "I have no idea," was the response.

"Why don't you get into this business?" Shanley asked. Then, Shanley opened the door in a couple of ways. First he sold the Browns and the radio station on Dieken's on-air potential. Then Shanley left for a job on the West Coast.

In 1985, the Browns had Jim Mueller and Nev Chandler alternating as play-by-play men, with Dieken doing color commentary. The next season, they paired Chandler and Dieken. Dieken has been on the radio ever since. His partners were Chandler and Casey Coleman until the team left for Baltimore after the 1995 season. Chandler and Coleman both died of cancer.

He was teamed up with Donovan when the team returned in 1999.

"Sometimes, it's more about timing than talent," said Dieken.

He was thinking about high school, how basketball turned into football. About the NFL, how he was dropped into the left tackle spot.

"I played next to two great guards—Gene Hickerson and later Robert Jackson," said Dieken. "That's what I mean about timing. Those guys really helped me."

Then broadcasting. As he had at left tackle, in radio he started at the pro level with zero experience. But that is at the heart of Dieken—the power of showing up. Doing the right thing, day after day, decade after decade.

"My father once told me that there will always be guys with more talent than you," said Dieken. "But you can outwork them."

After Dieken was drafted by the Browns, Charles Dieken told his son he'd give Dieken $100 if he ever made the Pro Bowl. It finally happened in his 10th pro season. Dieken called his dad, reminding him about the $100.

"That's good," said Charles Dieken. "Think you can do it again?"

Charles Dieken did not believe in handing out compliments—or money—frivolously.

Then Dieken told one more story.

"My brother Paul was in the Special Olympics and he loved it," said Dieken. "That got me interested in it."

Over the years, he's helped raise about $250,000 for the organization.

"One day, my brother won four ribbons and medals," said Dieken. "He got in the car, held them up to me and said, 'How do you like that, Hot Shot!'"

Dieken laughed as he told the story, one that says so much about him and his late brother.

SMALL, BUT SOLID: GREG PRUITT

Mention the name Greg Pruitt to most Browns fans, and they probably have heard of him. They know he was a pretty good running back. They may recall something about "tear-away" jerseys. That was when Pruitt wore thin shirts on the field. A defender would grab the jersey to try and drag down Pruitt . . .

But Pruitt was gone!

All the tackler had was a piece of jersey in his hand.

Eventually, those "tear-away" jerseys were outlawed by the NFL. But that image sticks to Pruitt, at least in the minds of some Browns fans.

There was so much more to Pruitt than gimmick jerseys. And the part about "a pretty good running back," also is selling Pruitt short. OK, bad pun there. Pruitt was listed at 5-foot-9 when he came out of Oklahoma. He was fast, but small. Too small. Supposedly would be too fragile for the NFL.

"All my life," Pruitt said. "I heard things like that all my life."

OK, the "too short" line is a lousy pun, but it goes to the heart of the Pruitt story. We shouldn't be talking about "tear-away" jerseys or his small stature. We should be talking about how Pruitt came to the Browns in 1973—it's a cool draft story. And we go right to the numbers.

After Pruitt was drafted, the Browns were in a major decline.

They fell from 7-5-2 in 1973 to 4-10 in 1974. The coach was the mediocre Nick Skorich. The front office generally drafted poorly. The quarterback was the overwhelmed Mike Phipps.

In the 1970s, Browns running backs rushed for at least 1,000 yards in a season only four times. Pruitt did it three times in a row: 1975, 1976 and 1977. The other was Mike Pruitt (no relation to Greg), who rushed for 1,294 yards.

In 1978, Greg Pruitt ran for 960 yards.

Pruitt is the last Cleveland Brown to have three consecutive 1,000-yard rushing seasons. Before that, you have to go back to Hall of Famers Jim Brown and Leroy Kelly to find such consistent and productive running backs.

"It's been like that all my life," said Pruitt. "Underrated."

* * *

When Greg Pruitt was a kid in Houston, he had a football hero. He told the story of watching the Browns one Sunday on his old black and white TV with some friends. They saw Jim Brown in a game against the Giants. Brown headed to the sideline. It looked like he would be tackled, so why not step out of bounds? Instead, Brown paused for a second, dropped his shoulder and drilled the tackler, knocking him flat.

Then Brown ran over another tackler, threw away a third and scored a touchdown.

"We went outside to play," said Pruitt. "We drew straws to see who'd get to be Jim Brown. My friend Charles won and got to be Brown."

Pruitt said Charles tried the same move as Brown, dropped his shoulder and tried to run over tacklers.

"A couple of us hit him," said Pruitt. "We played sandlot tackle football (no equipment). We broke both his arms and his leg."

Really?

Greg Pruitt was mostly a return man in his first two seasons (playing behind Ken Brown and an aging Leroy Kelly in the backfield). Given a chance to play near the end of the 1973 season, he made the most of it. Here, he runs away from the Detroit Lions in 1975. *Charles Harris / The Plain Dealer*

"Really," said Pruitt. "Many years later, I was playing golf with Jim Brown. I told him everyone I grew up with loved him except one guy."

Brown asked, "Who?"

Pruitt told Brown about Charles and what happened. There is a moral to this story:

"When I played, I ran to avoid people," said Pruitt. "I didn't want to get hit. I knew there was only one Jim Brown."

* * *

Pruitt was a great high school player—but small.

He was 5-foot-9 and about 140 pounds when recruited by Oklahoma. In his first season with the Sooners (1970), he was mostly a receiver. But in 1971, Oklahoma made Pruitt a featured back in coach Chuck Fairbanks' offense called the Wishbone-T.

He didn't just run, he blurred. One of his college coaches bought him a T-shirt that read HELLO on the front and GOODBYE on the back. That's how it was with the ball in Pruitt's hands.

HELLO . . . blink of an eye . . . GOODBYE.

He's gone!

He bolted for 18 touchdowns. He averaged 9.0 yards per carry. He ran for 294 yards in a single game.

On his practice helmet, he wrote the word SPOTLIGHT. That was his nickname in high school "because I was in it so much," as he told Sports Illustrated in 1972.

He also wore a sweatshirt with the letters UT—as in ULTIMATE TALENT.

In college, he sometimes signed autographs: "Greg Pruitt, The Breakaway Kid."

Pruitt was confident bordering on cocky, but that had to be the case. He had NFL dreams, wanting to support his mother who ran a beauty shop in Houston. He wore a large Afro and high-heeled shoes (this was the "cool" 1970s) to look a little taller off the field.

It didn't matter how many yards he gained or how many games his team won . . . Pruitt was supposedly too small to be a regular NFL running back.

In three seasons at Oklahoma, he averaged 7.5 yards per carry. And 15.0 yards per catch. He scored 39 touchdowns. He was a Consensus All-American in 1971 and 1972, his last two college seasons. (Pruitt would enter the College Football Hall of Fame in 1999.)

That had to be enough to be a first-round draft pick, or so Pruitt believed.

* * *

Imagine being an All-American for your college coach. And then, partly because of how well you played for him, your college coach receives an offer to become an NFL head coach—for the New England Patriots.

Next, imagine that coach having THREE first-round picks in the draft. You might easily go on to imagine your coach would want a record-breaking back from Oklahoma.

"I still can't believe he didn't draft me," said Pruitt.

Chuck Fairbanks had coached Pruitt during three seasons at Oklahoma. He left the 11-1 Oklahoma Sooners for the NFL. The Patriots had the fourth, 11th and 19th picks in the first round of the 1973 draft.

"I knew he'd take me with one of those picks," said Pruitt. "I just knew it."

Instead, Fairbanks selected Alabama guard John Hannah, USC running back Sam Cunningham and Purdue receiver Darryl Stingley. Watching his old college coach pick Cunningham was devastating to Pruitt.

"I knew I was a first-rounder," he said. "I played well enough to be a first-rounder. And my coach passed me up? Three times? I couldn't watch it any more."

Remember, the year was 1973. Pruitt wasn't exactly watching the draft. It wasn't televised.

"I was a journalism student," Pruitt said. "I was watching the wire (Associated Press) as the picks came up."

There were 26 picks in the first round of the 1973 draft. The Browns had two selections at 16 and 22. They went with Steve Holden, a wide receiver from Arizona State. At No. 22, it was USC guard Pete Adams. Those rank as two of the worst first-round picks in franchise history.

So even the Browns weren't that sold on Pruitt.

At the end of the first round, a discouraged and angry Pruitt left the journalism classroom and the Associated Press wire machine.

"I was just learning to play golf," he said. "I went to the course, the back nine, just to get away from everyone."

He was whacking away at a golf ball when he heard someone call his name.

"It was a reporter," said Pruitt. "He said Cleveland took me."

Pruitt's first thought was . . . Who? The Houston native had never heard from the Browns before the draft. He'd never been to Cleveland.

"I was still mad I didn't go in the first round," said Pruitt. "I was mad at my old coach for passing over me three times. Finally, I was glad someone took me."

* * *

"When I came to Cleveland they weighed me, and I hid a 5-pound weight by my foot," he said. "That got me up to 177 pounds."

He said he was 5-foot-10. Really?

"Might have been a stretch," said Pruitt. "But I was taller than Nick Skorich!"

Skorich was his first coach with the Browns in 1973.

"He was like 5-foot-7," said Pruitt. "Here he was, looking up to me and telling me I wasn't big enough to play."

Pruitt was mostly a return man in his first two seasons, playing behind Ken Brown and an aging Leroy Kelly in the backfield. Those two running backs combined to average only 3.2 yards per carry in 1973. Pruitt was given a chance to play near the end of the season and rushed for 110 yards vs. Kansas City. He also scored a winning touchdown in a game against Pittsburgh. Pruitt averaged 6.0 yards per carry in 1973.

For a long time, Browns owner Art Modell insisted he was the reason the Browns picked Pruitt in the second round. I often

Greg Pruitt, considered too small by many at the time of the draft, played 12 years in the NFL, nine with the Browns. Here, he shows reporters his scar after knee surgery in 1980. *Marvin M. Greene / The Plain Dealer*

wondered if that was an after-the-fact rewrite of history. But given how Skorich had so little interest in playing Pruitt—he thought the running back was too small, of course—the story of Modell pushing for Pruitt is probably true.

"Skorich didn't believe in me," said Pruitt. "But Forrest Gregg did."

Gregg was the Browns' offensive line coach in 1974. He became the Browns' head coach in 1975. That was the first of Pruitt's three consecutive 1,000-yard rushing seasons. Brian Sipe took over as starting quarterback. By 1978, Sam Rutigliano was the new coach and Pruitt had turned into a big-time running back.

Pruitt suffered a knee injury in 1979. That led to Mike Pruitt taking over as the featured running back. Greg Pruitt became an elite pass-catcher out of the backfield with 50 receptions in 1980 and 65 in 1981.

After the 1981 season, Pruitt was traded to Oakland. He was a superb return man for the Raiders, making a Pro Bowl as a special teams player at the age of 32.

He played 12 years in the NFL, nine with the Browns. He went to four Pro Bowls. He even threw six TD passes on halfback option plays. The most he ever made in a season was $320,000.

* * *

Pruitt remembered a couple things about playing against his old college coach and New England.

"We played him twice and beat him both times," said Pruitt. "Returned an 88-yard kickoff for a touchdown in one of those games."

In a 30-27 victory over Fairbanks and the Patriots, Pruitt rushed for 151 yards and caught four passes for 51 yards.

Pruitt said on his flight back to Oklahoma after his first meeting with the Browns, he was sitting in the back of the plane he caught in St. Louis. A flight attendant said someone in first class wanted to buy him a drink.

"I looked up there and saw it was Fairbanks," said Pruitt. "I said he could keep the drink."

That was 48 years ago.

"Turned out going to Cleveland was the best thing that ever

happened to me," said Pruitt. "I love the fans here. I live here. I've been involved in the community, done some media. People have been great to me."

One last fact about Pruitt.

Look at the list of all-time Browns running backs ranked by their rushing stats.

1. Jim Brown, 12,312 yards.
2. Leroy Kelly, 7,274 yards.
3. Mike Pruitt, 6,540 yards.
4. Greg Pruitt, 5,496 yards.

He stands tall on that list in Browns history.

WHAT MIGHT HAVE BEEN: THE KARDIAC KIDS

After a speaking engagement, I was handed a baggie containing small square pieces of orange and brown paper.

"What's this?" I asked.

"It's confetti," said the man who gave it to me.

I waited. He looked at me. I looked at the baggie.

"Confetti from what?" I asked.

"From the 'Red Right 88' game," he said. "I want you to have it."

I looked at it and laughed. Not at him. I understood. Only a Browns fan would save confetti from a 1981 playoff game loss and give it to a fellow Clevelander 38 years later.

On the baggie he had written: "February 7, 2021. Super Bowl 55. Cleveland 30, L.A. Rams 28." He was making a prediction that seemed like an outrageous dream at the time. But in the 2021 NFL playoffs, the Browns did knock off Pittsburgh in the first round. That was their first playoff victory since 1994. And it was the first since the team returned as an expansion franchise in 1999.

"I loved that team," said the fan.

He meant the 1980 Browns. He kept the confetti from the 14-12 loss to the Oakland Raiders on January 4, 1981, to prove the point.

Saving confetti from a loss says something about Cleveland fans of that era.

How about this: a quarterback who had a career 57-55 record as a starter with the Browns is still revered by many.

That's Brian Sipe.

And there are happy thoughts about a coach who had a 47-50 record with the Browns, yet is still respected.

That's Sam Rutigliano.

This was a "you-had-to-be-there" era for Browns fans. At its peak, in 1980, the team finished 11-5. They were called the Kardiac Kids.

According to Sipe's accounts in several interviews over the years, here's the basic version of how the 1980 Browns came to be called by that nickname. A doctor from the Cleveland Clinic came to the practice facility. He had a document from a cardiac machine showing how a patient died right in the middle of watching one of the Browns' nerve-rattling games that season.

Not sure if that's true, but it's a good—albeit rather ghoulish—story.

In the end, the veracity of the story doesn't matter. The Kardiac Kids nickname was perfect for Browns teams from both the 1979 and 1980 seasons.

The 1979 Browns were 9-7. They played three overtime games, winning two. Overall, they were 7-5 in games decided by seven points or fewer. They missed the playoffs along with three other teams that also had 9-7 records.

But the 1980 season would mark the third consecutive year of stability on the offensive coaching staff, with Rutigliano assisted by Jim Shofner, Jim Garrett, Rich Kotite and Rod Humenuik. Joined that year by Paul Hackett, they also were working with the same key skill position players led by Sipe.

The year did not start off previewing any of the excitement that was to come. The Browns were 1-3 in the exhibition season and then lost the first two games of the regular season.

Then they caught fire, winning 11 of the next 14. They were 9-3 in games decided by seven points or less. Their 11-5 record tied them with the Houston Oilers for first place in the AFC Central Division and they won the tiebreaker for the title based on an AFC record of 8-4 compared with Houston's 7-5 mark.

Researching details on the Browns' 1980 season, I found a story by Sports Illustrated magazine's Paul Zimmerman, one of the greatest football writers ever.

"They struggle," was how Zimmerman opened his story of the Browns beating the New York Jets 17-14 with two games remaining in the season.

"They make dull games exciting," wrote Zimmerman. "Why? Well, no one has quite figured out the Cleveland Browns, but whatever else they may be, the Browns are also 10-4 and sitting alone at the top of the AFC Central.... Not a bad record for a team picked to finish third at best in a division that has been the property of Pittsburgh and Houston the last few years."

Zimmerman pointed out how the Browns "have the AFC's second-worst defense." He added they also have "as sophisticated a passing game as there is in the NFL."

In the rear-view mirror of time, this was a pretty good team that overachieved and had a little luck for those two seasons.

But most of all, they were wildly entertaining. With Sipe, they had an underdog for a quarterback. In Rutigliano, they had a fast-talking, engaging coach who was a natural risk-taker from Brooklyn, New York.

Rutigliano came to his first NFL head coaching position with the philosophy of throwing the ball. He had worked as an assistant on offense in three of his four NFL coaching jobs from 1967-77 before getting the Browns' job. In a press conference back then he said, "Fasten your seat belt. I like to throw... I'll go for it on fourth down—from anywhere on the field."

* * *

In Cleveland, Rutigliano found a soulmate in Sipe, whose presence in an NFL uniform defied the odds. In college, at San Diego State, Sipe had enjoyed two remarkably similar seasons as a junior and senior in 1970 and 1971. As a junior, he completed 58% of 337 pass attempts for 2,618 yards with 23 touchdowns and 20 interceptions. As a senior, he completed 53.1% of 369 attempts for 2,532 yards with 17 touchdowns and 21 interceptions.

Browns coach Nick Skorich told the Akron Beacon Journal after the 1972 draft that the team liked that Sipe played "in a drop-back offense," throwing 30 to 40 passes per game.

Sipe's college coach was ahead of his time in developing the passing game as the modern way to win. He was Don Coryell, whose offense was nicknamed "Air Coryell" as he enjoyed later NFL success in both St. Louis and San Diego.

"The Browns drafted me in the 13th round in 1972," said Sipe. "I never thought I'd last. I already had another job lined up when I went to training camp."

What was that?

"I was going to move to Steamboat Springs (Colorado) and be a waiter," he said. "I was going to ski all day with some friends who were working in restaurants there."

Sipe told me that story a few years ago. It made sense to have a backup plan for his life. He was the 330th pick in that draft, which lasted 17 rounds overall. Other than Sipe and first-round pick Thom Darden, it wasn't much of a draft for the Browns.

"I was a beach kid from Southern California," he said. "I wasn't even supposed to make the team. No one was anxious for me to play. For the first two years, I was on the taxi squad. I wore a baseball cap, a sweatsuit and held a clipboard."

In Sipe's rookie year, the Browns were 10-4. The starting quarterback was Mike Phipps, who was the opposite of Sipe. The

Browns had traded future Hall of Famer Paul Warfield to Miami for the rights to Phipps. He had been a star at Purdue and was the No. 3 overall pick. He was a gifted, natural athlete with a 6-foot-3, 210-pound build and a rocket launcher for an arm. But Phipps wasn't an accurate passer and didn't seem to have the same football acumen as Sipe, who was generously listed at 6-foot-1 and had so-so arm strength.

"I rarely played in practice in my first two seasons," Sipe said. "When I did get in there, it was near the end and I usually fumbled."

Sipe can be self-effacing. He must have shown something for the Browns to keep him around. In 1974, Phipps was injured during the season. Sipe started five games and the Browns went 2-3. He threw one TD pass compared with seven interceptions. He fumbled eight times, losing four. That meant he had 11 turnovers compared to that one TD pass.

Yikes!

But Phipps also had problems that year. He completed only 45.7% of his passes, with nine touchdowns compared with 17 interceptions. The Browns had become a lousy team. Their record dropped from 10-4 in 1972 to 7-5-2 in 1973 and 4-10 in 1974. Then owner Art Modell made a coaching change, promoting offensive line coach Forrest Gregg to replace Skorich. Gregg had been praised during his playing career at Green Bay by the late Packers head coach Vince Lombardi.

In Gregg's first year, the Browns started the season with nine consecutive losses. Phipps was the starter at quarterback but Sipe did get two starts (both losses). The Browns finished 3-11.

So after his first four years in the NFL, Sipe had started seven games. His team had won two of them. He had thrown a pair of TD passes compared with 10 interceptions. It's remarkable that he was around for a fifth season.

* * *

When Gregg and Modell had a falling out in 1977, Rutigliano was hired as head coach for 1978. He immediately committed to Sipe. At that point, Sipe had been through five offensive coordinators between 1972 and 1977.

"Sam called me in and told me I was going to be his quarterback," Sipe told Zimmerman. "He said we were going to throw the ball and throw it on first down and from anywhere on the field. He said I'd call the plays, unless I showed I couldn't handle it."

That was Rutigliano's best move, putting faith and trust in Sipe. That wasn't easy in 1978. But there was something he saw in Sipe that appealed to Rutigliano's judgment about people.

Yes, Sipe was intelligent—a critical attribute for a quarterback who has to remember plays along with studying and dissecting opposing defenses.

Yes, he had poise, not breaking down emotionally even when taking a physical beating on some of those lousy Browns teams in the mid-1970s.

But there was more.

Perhaps Rutigliano saw a little of himself in Sipe.

The coach wasn't a hot commodity coming into the NFL. He didn't play in the pros. He spent eight years as a high school coach before finally moving into the college ranks. He spent 11 years as an NFL assistant. He never had been an NFL team coordinator. When Modell hired him, Rutigliano was coming from serving two seasons as wide receivers coach for New Orleans—where the Saints had a 7-21 record in those years.

Modell, a New Yorker, seemed to have an immediate kinship with the loquacious Rutigliano, who also made decisions from the heart. This was his guy—and his kind of guy.

The Plain Dealer sportswriter Chuck Heaton broke the story of Rutigliano being hired. The response in Cleveland was, Sam who?

Sam and Sipe?

On paper in 1978, it didn't seem like it was going to be a winning combination.

But then it worked.

I'm going back to what Sports Illustrated's Zimmerman wrote in 1980 because he captured the aura of the Browns that season.

"The biggest mistake coaches make is saying, 'We're going to establish the run' or 'establish the pass,' " Rutigliano told Zimmerman. "You try to establish first downs. You keep the ball moving. And the clock. You do it in the most intelligent way you can."

You also can add the word "entertaining" to that description. That's my adjective, not Zimmerman's. But it's a major part of the Sipe legend that lingers today, 40-plus years later, for Browns fans who lived through that era.

"Daring, yes," wrote Zimmerman. "But (Sipe is) always operating from a very high plane of intelligence; he has the lowest interception rate of any quarterback in the NFL. Sipe is not imposing-looking as NFL specimens go: a shade over 6-feet, slim build, almost frail-looking. Quiet, thoughtful, but with inner fires that have made him the league's ultimate come-from-behind quarterback."

In an interview with Cleveland Magazine after the 1980 season, Sipe said this: "I was not burdened by the great expectations that a lot of other quarterbacks had to deal with . . . I kind of enjoy the label (as a lucky overachiever)—that I'm the guy whose arm isn't quite strong enough or that I am not quite big enough . . . "

That is part of what made the Kardiac Kids so endearing to the fans.

In their first three years together, Sam and Sipe had records of 8-8, 9-7 and 11-5. Rutigliano won a Coach of the Year award in both the 1979 and 1980 seasons.

Rutigliano and Browns general manager Peter Hadhazy had a

tremendous 1978 draft when they used their two first-round picks on linebacker Clay Matthews and tight end Ozzie Newsome.

In 1980, they relied on running back Mike Pruitt as he rushed for 1,034 yards. The other 1980 leaders on offense were excellent receivers Reggie Rucker and Dave Logan. They used Greg Pruitt coming out of the backfield as a receiver. Those four players and Newsome each had 50 receptions or more. Another backup running back, Calvin Hill, was the team leader in receptions for touchdowns with six. Backup receiver Ricky Feacher had only 10 catches for the year, but four went for touchdowns. Sipe won the NFL's Most Valuable Player award, completing 61% of his passes (very good for that era), including 30 for touchdowns with 14 interceptions. Sipe's passing yards totaled 4,132. At that time, it was the second-highest single-season amount in NFL history.

The Browns' offense also compiled these NFL league-wide accomplishments:

- 2nd in passing yardage
- 2nd in fewest sacks (23)
- 2nd (tied) in pass completion percentage (60.8)
- 3rd (tied) in fewest interceptions (14)
- 5th in total yards per game on offense
- 8th in points per game

"We had an awesome offense," said Newsome, looking back 41 years later. "And the city embraced us. Cleveland was coming out of going bankrupt (the city government was defaulting on short-term loans) and the Cuyahoga River catching fire in the 1970s. The fans were so excited to have something good bringing attention to their town."

* * *

Then came "Red Right 88."

The Browns faced Oakland in the divisional round of the playoffs. Oakland had defeated Houston 27-7 in the wild-card round. The game time temperature at Municipal Stadium was 4 degrees above zero. The wind chill was minus 36. It was the second-coldest NFL game on record up until then.

A whipping wind off Lake Erie was a huge factor. Players' hands were frozen. The football felt like an ice ball.

All of those things affected both the Raiders and the Browns, and especially Cleveland kicker Don Cockroft.

Cockroft had already been dealing with major back problems and sciatica issues during the season. Later, he learned he had two herniated disks. Cockroft was 16-of-26 (61.5%) on field goal attempts for the season. He had missed two field goals against Denver and three against Pittsburgh. The Browns lost 19-16 to Denver and 16-13 to the Steelers. So ups and downs had been part of Cockroft's year.

Against the Raiders, Cockroft missed field goal tries from 30 and 47 yards. Another kick failed when backup quarterback and holder Paul McDonald dropped the center snap. McDonald wore gloves during the kicking attempts.

Cockroft had converted two field goals in the third quarter—both in the closed end of the Stadium, so the windy conditions were not as prominent. The misses and dropped snap were in the open end . . . and that's where the Browns were driving in the fourth quarter with the game on the line.

For a wide-open passing team such as the 1980 Browns, these were the worst possible conditions for a game. Sipe had trouble hanging onto the frozen football. He fumbled four times, losing two.

The Browns trailed 14-12 with 49 seconds left. They had driven from their 15-yard line to the Raiders' 13 in 1:33, in nine plays. At

The Kardiac Kids nickname was perfect for Browns teams from both the 1979 and 1980 seasons. *C.H. Pete Copeland / The Plain Dealer*

this point, Sipe was 13-of-39 passing with two interceptions, no touchdowns, and he had been sacked twice.

It was second down and 9 yards to go. Conventional wisdom was for Rutigliano to run the ball, chew up the clock, then kick a field goal to win 15-14.

Cockroft said in a 1999 interview with Akron Beacon Journal

The end of the Kardiac Kids: "Red Right 88." On Jan. 4, 1981, Oakland's Mike Davis intercepts a Brian Sipe pass intended for Ozzie Newsome (82) with 49 seconds remaining in the game. *George Heinz / The Plain Dealer*

pro football writer Patrick McManamon that he told Sipe to get the ball on the right hash mark on the field, because the wind was going right to left.

But Rutigliano (although he never said so) trusted Sipe more than Cockroft at this point.

Rutigliano called "Red Right 88."

In 1999, McManamon recounted the story of the play and detailed the assignments. "Red" was the formation.

1. "Right" assigned the position of the receiver known as the "Y" (in this case, Reggie Rucker). The receiver known as the "X" would go to the left side.

2. "88" described the protection for Sipe.

3. The full name of the play, McManamon reported, was, "Red slot right, halfback stay, 88."

4. "Halfback stay" meant that the two running backs—Cleo Miller and Mike Pruitt—stayed in the backfield for protection for Sipe. But, McManamon wrote, when Sipe got to the huddle, the formation he called had Newsome inside Rucker on the right and Logan on the left. The way Rutigliano had said the words on the sideline, Logan and Rucker would have been on the right and Newsome would have been on the left.

Rutigliano said later it wasn't the exact matchup he wanted but he thought it was OK because the Raiders' Dwayne O'Steen would be the defender on Logan.

Rucker told McManamon the play was part of the Browns' "base" pass offense and had been run "many, many" times during the year.

Rucker and Newsome would be running post-patterns. Mike Pruitt was available for a short safety-valve pass.

Finally, all this action was to create a diversion for Logan to be open in the end zone. That's how Rutigliano described it to me in 2010.

During the timeout before the play, Rutigliano told Sipe, "Throw it into Lake Erie if no one is open."

Sipe also remembered Rutigliano saying, "Don't take a sack," because that would make an already challenging field goal even harder. Sipe said that was his primary concern, not being sacked. He wasn't going to be patient in the pocket. If he spotted someone open, he was throwing it.

"Logan actually was open," Rutigliano said. "But Brian saw Ozzie and threw it to him first. I never blamed Brian. He made great decisions all season. You had to trust him."

Oakland safety Mike Davis stepped in front of Newsome and caught the pass. Interception. Game over.

"Sam took the entire blame for the call, but I threw the ball," Sipe has often said.

When Oakland went on to win the Super Bowl, defeating Philadelphia 27-10, the Raiders became the first wild card entry ever to win the championship.

Looking back, "Red Right 88" was the day the Kardiac Kids brand name became a flat-liner.

"We've lived and died with the pass all year long," Newsome told reporters after the game. "This time, we died."

All that the frozen fans could do was trudge out of the silent Stadium, wondering what would have happened if Cockroft had attempted the field goal.

All the fans except one, who bent down on the cold concrete to scoop up some confetti to save for the day a title would come to Cleveland.

THE LAST HALL OF FAMER: OZZIE NEWSOME

I recently wondered: Who is the last Hall of Famer to be drafted by the Browns?

Gene Hickerson, Paul Warfield, Leroy Kelly and Clay Matthews came to mind. Matthews because he should be in the Hall of Fame, but keeps coming up short in the votes.

Finally, I looked it up.

Ozzie Newsome.

That's the same Ozzie Newsome who was picked in the same 1978 draft as Matthews.

Hickerson was the last Cleveland Brown to be enshrined in the Hall of Fame, in 2007, but he was a seventh-round pick in 1957. Newsome entered the Hall of Fame in 1999.

* * *

In 1978, no one knew Ozzie Newsome Jr. would be a Hall of Famer, of course. Or that he would change how pro football viewed the tight end position.

He was a wide receiver at Alabama, where Coach Paul "Bear" Bryant ran the wishbone, run-driven offense and rarely threw the ball.

Newsome decided to play for Bryant after being an All-State

receiver at Colbert County High in Leighton, Alabama. He was at the center of a recruiting war between Auburn and Alabama.

Auburn's appeal was an offense that threw the ball.

And Alabama? It was Bryant and his legendary status in the state. It also was Bryant's accent on team first and winning. At Alabama, the biggest thing was the program. The SEC titles and a chance to win the national title.

Newsome went to Alabama because he wanted to be part of something special.

Alabama remained a ground-driven team, but Newsome excelled when the Crimson Tide did throw him the ball. He was a first-team All-American in 1977, and the SEC Player of the Year in his final two years for the Crimson Tide.

How good was Newsome?

Bryant called Newsome, "The greatest end in Alabama history . . . a total team player, fine blocker, outstanding leader, great receiver with concentration, speed and hands."

He also could play tight end or wide receiver. He didn't start his first game at Alabama, but entered after one play. Bryant liked what saw of the freshman, and Newsome started every game after that for four years.

Newsome caught only 36 passes as a senior. No surprise because Alabama ran the run-heavy wishbone offense. They completed only 71 passes all season. Newsome averaged 22.3 yards per reception as a 6-foot-2, 210-pounder.

Alabama had a 42-6 record in Newsome's four years.

* * *

In 1978, no one knew this young man would one day become a general manager in the National Football League. But now, when you listen to Newsome looking back at the first round of the 1978 draft, you realize he was already doing his own mock draft.

Ozzie Newsome leaves the field after a game in 1988. "He can catch a BB in the dark," Browns coach Sam Rutigliano said about Newsome on draft day.
Curt Chandler / The Plain Dealer

"Before the draft, I knew who was going to pick receivers," said Newsome in 2021. "The Saints were going to take one. Green Bay was probably going to take one. San Diego and Cleveland also were looking at receivers. I figured I was going to one of those teams."

In fact, Newsome had a feeling his pro future was in Cleveland.

"The Browns had two picks in the first round," he said.

Then Newsome told a story about the Browns and his Alabama roommate, running back Johnny Davis.

"I went to the Senior Bowl," said Newsome. "Back then, they didn't have Pro Days. Teams just sent scouts and assistant coaches to the campus to work you out."

Alabama was a prime stop, and not just because of Newsome. Davis, with whom he shared an apartment, was considered a top running back prospect.

"It seemed every day someone wanted me to work out," said Newsome. "They wanted to time you in the 40 (yard dash). They wanted you to catch passes, run routes . . . things like that. I was getting burned out."

Someone from the Browns called their apartment, wanting Davis and Newsome to work out. Newsome was done with all the workouts. He was skipping it. Davis went and worked out with Browns receivers coach Rich Kotite.

Afterward, Davis called Newsome and asked him to come down and meet the guy from Cleveland.

"I don't want to work out," said Newsome.

Kotite grabbed the phone and said, "I want you to catch a few balls. I just want to look at you."

Newsome went to the football complex. Kotite asked Newsome to sit down. They made small talk for a few minutes.

"That's all I need," said Kotite.

"OK," said Newsome, going back to his apartment.

* * *

The night before the draft, Newsome received calls from several teams. They wanted him to know they might draft him—and to stay by the phone in the first round.

The same was true for Davis, his roommate.

"Johnny got frustrated with the entire draft process," said Newsome. "He went to his home in Montgomery. So I stayed in the apartment, alone."

Davis would be picked in the second round by Tampa Bay. The fullback would later play for the Browns from 1982-87. His nickname was "B-1" as in B-1 Bomber, for his blocking ability.

"Everyone knew Earl Campbell was going No. 1 to Houston," said Newsome. "Art Still went No. 2 to Kansas City. The Saints took (receiver) Wes Chandler."

Newsome mentioned receiver James Lofton going No. 6 to Green Bay, then tight end Ken MacAfee No. 7 to San Francisco.

"Cleveland had the No. 12 pick," said Newsome. "I thought I'd go there."

Instead, the Browns took linebacker Clay Matthews, of USC.

"Then San Diego took (receiver) John Jefferson (at No. 14)," said Newsome. "I was getting frustrated. I remember my Alabama teammate (tackle) Bob Cryder went to New England at No. 18."

Forty-three years after the draft, Newsome remembered all this—correctly.

"The Browns had the 20th pick," he said. "I figured that was my best shot (to be taken in the first round)."

* * *

If you connect all the dots from the deals, the Browns trading Hall of Famer Paul Warfield led to Hall of Famer Ozzie Newsome.

In 1970, as the draft approached, the Browns were desperate for a quarterback. They had aging Bill Nelsen and his cranky knees. They became infatuated with Purdue quarterback Mike Phipps.

The Browns projected they could add Phipps with the No. 3 pick in that draft, which belonged to Miami. They sent their star receiver Warfield to the Dolphins for the third pick—and selected Phipps.

For a long time, the deal was a disaster for Cleveland. The Browns were 24-25-2 with Phipps as a starter. At times, they won in spite of him. Phipps completed only 48% of his passes in seven years with a frightening 40-to-81 ratio of TD passes to interceptions.

But the Browns suddenly got lucky. Heading into the 1978 draft, Chicago was searching for a quarterback. The Bears offered their first-round pick for Phipps. Brian Sipe had emerged as the Browns starting quarterback, so the Browns didn't need to select a quarterback. They made the deal and had the No. 20 pick in the draft.

* * *

But the Browns didn't use the No. 20 pick on Ozzie Newsome.

Newsome's phone finally rang. It was Art Modell.

"Is this Ozzie Newsome?" asked the Browns owner.

"Yes sir," said Newsome.

"We had the 20th pick and we traded back, hoping you'll still be there," said Modell. "We knew you weren't going to be taken at 21. Not sure about 22. We're just giving you a call."

The three players picked in front of Newsome were running back Elvis Peacock (20), defensive end Randy Holloway (21) and defensive back Ron Johnson (22).

"At that point, I just wanted someone to take me," said Newsome. "I didn't care."

The phone rang again. It was Modell.

"We're on the clock," said the owner. "You're a Cleveland Brown."

Newsome was relieved and joyous at the same time. But it was unlike today when players have draft parties at their homes or favorite restaurants or even travel to the site of the draft where their selection is announced on TV.

Newsome was alone.

"After I got the call from Art, I called my parents to tell them," Newsome said. "My mother had two sisters and a brother living in Cleveland, so I had been there before."

The Browns wanted him to come to Cleveland immediately for a rookie mini-camp.

"But I was set to graduate," said Newsome. "I was going to be the first one in our family to get a degree, and my parents wanted to watch me walk across the stage and get my diploma."

Ozzie Newsome announces his retirement in 1991. As a tight end, he was one of his team's most-targeted receivers during an era when that was unusual. *Andrew Cifranic / The Plain Dealer*

New Browns coach Sam Rutigliano allowed Newsome to report the following week.

The Browns had dropped from No. 20 to No. 23 in the draft. They added a fourth round pick in the process.

"As a GM, I know now that's a good deal," said Newsome.

After selecting Newsome, there was a celebration with the Browns front office and coaching staff.

Remember that trip to Alabama by Browns assistant Rich Kotite? When Kotite was satisfied just to meet Newsome in person?

"I wanted to see if he had a big butt," Rutigliano said on draft day. "I wanted him to weigh 230-240 pounds. I couldn't tell on film. So I sent Rich Kotite to take a look at the size of his rear end. I liked everything else about Newsome."

Kotite said all was well when it came to Newsome, from the front and behind.

"He can catch a BB in the dark," Rutigliano also said on draft day.

Newsome still recalls his rookie contract: a $100,000 signing bonus. That was the only guaranteed money. He received three non-guaranteed seasons: $50,000; $57,500 and $65,000.

* * *

When Newsome arrived at training camp, Kotite was waiting for him.

"Sam wants to see you," said the assistant coach. "Don't worry, nothing is wrong."

Newsome went into Rutigliano's office.

"There's no doubt you can be a wide receiver in this league," said the coach. "But we want you to be a tight end. And we're moving you to tight end because we're going to throw you the football. With some of the pass coverages teams are playing now, you'll be a mismatch."

"OK," said Newsome, but there must have been some doubt in his voice.

"Ozzie, we are going to throw you the football," repeated Rutigliano.

The young man from Muscle Shoals, Alabama, played 13 years for the Browns. He never missed a game. He caught 662 passes, made three Pro Bowls and was voted into the Hall of Fame in 1999.

In 2010, Peter King (then with Sports Illustrated) named Newsome the No. 6 tight end in NFL history.

"One of the first flex players—a hybrid receiver and tight end—Newsome was his team's most important target for several years. He had back-to-back 89-catch seasons in 1983 and 1984."

This was back when tight ends were afterthoughts in most

passing offenses, not primary targets. Newsome changed some of that thinking.

In 1999, Sports Illustrated picked the 50 Greatest Sports Figures From Alabama.

Here's the top 10: 1) Hank Aaron. 2) Willie Mays. 3) Bo Jackson. 4) Ozzie Newsome. 5) Willie McCovey. 6) Satchel Paige. 7) John Hannah. 8) Bart Starr. 9) Charles Barkley. 10) Early Wynn.

Newsome later went on to become the first African-American with the title of general manager in NFL history. He ran the Baltimore Ravens for 24 years.

But it all started in Cleveland.

"Cleveland believed in me before I believed in me," said Newsome. "They gave me an opportunity to show my abilities, especially my strength in the passing game. The fans were great to me. It will always be a special place."

THE DEPARTURE OF BRIAN SIPE

It was painful.

The 1980 Kardiac Kids were 11-5. The next season, they were talking Super Bowl.

Instead, the Browns were 5-11 in 1981.

"It was a shock," said Kevin Byrne. "No one saw that coming. I was hired right before the 1981 season and I thought I was going to a team on the verge of a Super Bowl."

Byrne was hired as the team's public relations director. A Cleveland native and St. Edward graduate, he had worked in public relations with the old St. Louis (football) Cardinals. He was thrilled to come home.

"It was a year where about everything went wrong," said Byrne. "The biggest surprise for me was Brian Sipe, who was the MVP in 1980. He wasn't a big guy and he didn't have a great arm to begin with. But you could tell something was wrong, he was floating the ball at that time."

By 1981, Sipe was in his eighth pro season. Who knows how many concussions he'd had, because they were rarely diagnosed back then. He'd played all 16 games each season from 1978-81. He was sacked an average of 32 times per season. And back then they didn't count how many times the quarterback was knocked down after he threw a pass.

Generously listed at 6-foot-1 and 195 pounds, Sipe was surprisingly durable during those seasons. But the physical pounding caught up with him in 1981.

Sipe went from 30 touchdown passes and 14 interceptions in his 1980 MVP season to 17 touchdown passes and a league-high 25 interceptions in 1981.

He lost one fumble in 1980 . . . four in 1981. Adding up Sipe's interceptions and fumbles, he committed 29 turnovers in 1981.

After the 1981 regular season, Browns owner Art Modell invited Byrne and his wife Sally to watch a playoff game at the house of the owner.

In the middle of a mundane conversation, Modell suddenly looked at Byrne and asked, "What do you think of the way Brian Sipe plays?"

Now, Byrne would know better than to answer that question. He's in public relations, not player evaluation. But he was flattered the owner wanted to know his opinion on an important subject such as the team's quarterback.

"I was kind of surprised his arm wasn't as strong as I thought it was watching him on TV (in 1980)," said Byrne. "He can't get the ball out, especially when throwing deep. There were times when I looked at him and thought, 'I can throw it as well as he can.' "

Coach Sam Rutigiliano and his wife came in to join them not long after Byrne gave his assessment.

"Sam," said Modell. "Kevin kind of agrees with me about Brian."

Rutigliano gave Byrne a stony stare.

"Kevin thinks he can throw the ball as well as Brian some times," said Modell.

"Art, I didn't say exactly that," said Byrne.

Just then, the food was served. As the couple got up to go eat, Rutigliano gave a nod and looked in the direction of the kitchen—away from everyone else.

Byrne followed the coach into the kitchen.

"DON'T YOU EVER DO THAT TO ME AGAIN!" said a steaming Rutigliano.

"Sam, I had learned my lesson even before you brought it up now," said Byrne. "I didn't think he cared what I thought."

"No, no, NO!" said Rutigliano. "He looks for allies and then he teams up with them."

Byrne was right . . . and wrong.

His assessment of Sipe was correct. The quarterback had lost arm strength, possibly due to injuries. The Browns ended that 1981 season with five consecutive losses. Sipe was sacked 18 times in that stretch and threw 11 interceptions.

But Byrne learned another hard lesson. Modell loved to solicit opinions from everyone, often giving too much weight to people who knew too little about the situation—especially if those opinions agreed with those of the owner.

"That team had talent on offense," said former Browns GM Ernie Accorsi. "But overall, the team wasn't that good. Weak on the lines. Weak on defense. It began to show up."

Accorsi was with the Colts in the 1970s and early 1980s. He wasn't hired by the Browns until 1984, and then began as general manager in 1985.

But his opinion was correct. Rutigliano had a finesse team. All teams are quarterback-driven to some extent, and that's especially true when a team relies on its offense. Sipe was 32 in 1981 and had been through a lot physically and emotionally in the NFL.

In 1982, the Browns were 4-5 in a strike-shortened season. Sipe was benched in favor of Paul McDonald for the final three games of the season. They went 2-1 with McDonald, but the lefty quarterback from USC completed only 49% of his passes, with eight interceptions compared to only five touchdowns. So there was nothing special about his play.

Brian Sipe leaves the field after leading the Browns to a 31-7 victory over the Bengals on Nov. 23, 1980. He left the Browns for the USFL after the 1983 season. *Richard T. Conway / The Plain Dealer*

In 1983, Sipe had a bounce-back season. The Browns were 9-7. Sipe threw 26 TD passes vs. 23 interceptions. But he was coming to the end of his contract. And the rival United States Football League was trying to sign NFL players.

The New Jersey Generals were owned by a young real estate tycoon named Donald Trump. He went hard after Sipe, negotiating with the quarterback during the Browns' season. Sipe upset the Browns front office and coaching staff when he visited with Trump during the season. He made an oral agreement to change leagues on November 22, 1983. The Browns had four games left.

Sipe was paid $310,000 by the Browns in 1983. Trump agreed to pay Sipe $2 million over three years, fully guaranteed. The Browns wouldn't come close to those guaranteed dollars.

Now 34, Sipe knew he had one last chance to cash in as his body was breaking down.

Two days after Sipe's oral agreement, it was Thanksgiving. The Browns were 7-5 and had won 3-of-4 games. Rutigliano was not thrilled with the play of the team and had a very physical practice.

It was a long, cold, gray, dreary day. It was a chilled-to-the-bone afternoon, especially because the players wanted to be home with their families.

The coach brought the team together and told the players, "This is a great day. Thanksgiving is special. Make sure you reach out to your family today. If your family is with you, you are fortunate, I hope you all have a great day, a great Thanksgiving."

At this point, it was about 2:30 p.m. Much of Thanksgiving was over. The players were angry, and it was odd how Rutigliano misread the mood of his team.

When Rutigliano finished, Doug Dieken spoke up.

"Coach," said the offensive lineman. "By a vote of 23-22, we wish you a happy Thanksgiving, too."

That brought a laugh from the players, the first smiles of the day. At that point, Dieken was 34 years old. It was his 13th NFL season. He was one of the team leaders, and his pointed humor delivered a message: All was not well with the Browns.

MORE THAN A GLEAM: MARTY SCHOTTENHEIMER

When former Browns coach Marty Schottenheimer died on February 18, 2021, many Browns fans thought of a few words . . .

"There's a gleam, men . . . There's a gleam."

Schottenheimer was talking about the Lombardi championship trophy, the reflection of the light . . . the gleam.

In the end, Marty—that's how fans thought of him, only the first name—never experienced The Gleam. He coached for 21 years and never grasped the Super Bowl trophy.

Twenty-one years . . . only two losing seasons.

Twenty-one years . . . 13 trips to the playoffs.

Twenty-one years . . . a career record of 200-126-1.

Four-plus years as the Browns head coach . . . and The Gleam.

I believe The Gleam, for Marty, was far more than a reflection off a trophy. To Marty, football was more than a trophy. "Martyball" was more than a power-running attack and a physical defense.

To Marty, "The Gleam" was the look in the eyes of his players when they were coming together as a team. It's the wide eyes, not scared, but determined. It's the eyes saying, "I won't back down."

Or maybe, "If I get knocked down, I'll get back up."

Players such as Bernie Kosar, Kevin Mack and others recalled occasional tears in the eyes of Marty as he spoke to his teams before and after some games. Sometimes tears of joy, other times of pain.

But one thing never changed: This was a man with a rusty-bucket-of-nails toughness. This was a coach who sometimes screamed at his team, "Hit 'em! Pound 'em. Grind 'em into the dirt!" . . .

This was a man who was not afraid to cry in front of other men.

This was a man from Western Pennsylvania, the town of McDonald not far from Pittsburgh. The streets were brick. There was only one stop light. Most men worked in the coal mines or steel mills. It could have been Northeast Ohio. Same kind of no-nonsense, no-frills, no expectation of being given a free ride. It was dirt-under-the-fingernails, calloused hands and football as the great escape from the mines, mills and factories.

Browns Hall of Famer Lou Groza grew up in a place like that, Martins Ferry on the Ohio River. He once told me how his father said the soot on the windows "meant money." It came from the nearby mills, and pollution was the price you paid for good jobs. It also was a driving force for some young people to find a different life.

While Marty always was positive about his family and his hometown, he wanted more. He played well enough to earn a scholarship to nearby University of Pittsburgh.

That was where he was good, but not great—unless you measured the effort. He was drafted by the Buffalo Bills of the old American Football League in 1965. He made the AFL's Pro Bowl team as a rookie, as a special teams player. Special teams is where you have to sacrifice your body and your pride. It's football's version of the cleanup crew. You're not noticed unless you mess up.

Marty played six years with the Bills and Patriots and started a grand total of 11 games. He sweated out more than a few final cuts.

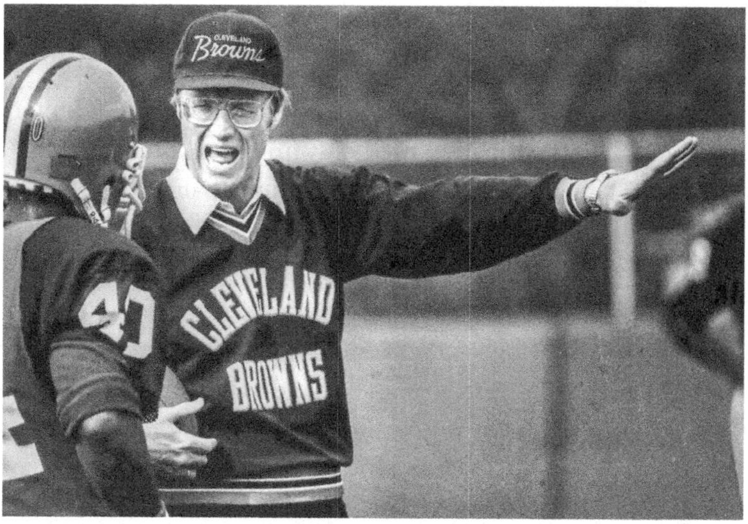

Marty Schottenheimer conducts his first practice as head coach of the Browns in 1984. *Chris Stephens / The Plain Dealer*

"I first met Marty in 1971," said Ernie Accorsi, who would later be Schottenheimer's GM in Cleveland.

Accorsi was the public relations director for the old Baltimore Colts. They had just picked up Schottenheimer on waivers from the Steelers, where he was told he was not going to make the team. It was still in training camp. Accorsi also was in charge of all room assignments on the road for the players.

"The guys were in line to get their room keys at the hotel," said Accorsi. "Marty stood in front of me. I wasn't sure who he was, just a new player who showed up."

According to Accorsi, here's what happened:

"What's your name?" asked Accorsi.

"You don't know me?" said Schottenheimer.

"Look, there are four future Hall of Famers in this line and you're holding it up," said Accorsi. "Either you tell me your name and I'll give you a key, or you can go get a room somewhere else."

"Schottenheimer," he said.

Accorsi handed him the key.

"A few days later, I got a call saying we were cutting Schottenheimer," said Accorsi. "That was it. My first encounter with him."

Accorsi laughed as he told the story more than 50 years after it happened.

* * *

When his playing career ended, Schottenheimer started a career in real estate. But the man who did everything with passion that at times bordered on desperation had little fire for selling houses. In his book "Martyball," written with Jeffrey Flanagan, Marty said there was a point when his wife Pat was working in a doctor's office, he couldn't find a steady job, and family members sent money to help with bills.

He missed football.

At the age of 31, he found a job with the Portland Storm of the World Football League. He was a linebackers coach for a team that couldn't pay its bills or coaches salaries. He was out of work at the end of the 1974 season.

Back home. Back to feeling dead inside. Back to wondering how he ever ended up away from the one thing that made him feel the most alive—football.

Marty eventually got a chance to do some scouting reports for the New York Giants. That led to a job on the team's defensive coaching staff in 1975. He was in the NFL. He was back in the game.

And within two years, he was the defensive coordinator of the Giants. By 1980, he had moved to Cleveland in that same position.

It was a remarkable rise, but memories of life on the bottom continued to fuel him. It's also why he hated when players took football for granted. Keep in mind that his career was in the old

AFL before the two leagues merged in 1970. To the young Marty, the NFL was a special place, a place that would probably always be out of his reach.

* * *

How did Schottenheimer end up as head coach of the Browns?

It was an act of desperation by team owner Art Modell. Schottenheimer had been the Browns defensive coordinator starting in 1980 under head coach Sam Rutigliano. The Browns had winning seasons in 1980 and 1983.

"I joined the Browns in 1984," said Accorsi. "I hadn't been around Marty since that meeting in Baltimore. Now, I saw him up close (as defensive coordinator). On the team plane after games, I saw several of the coaches having a beer and relaxing. Marty would have none of that. He'd be working at his seat. At this point, Marty was known as a guy who'd eventually be a good head coach."

The Browns opened that 1984 season with a 1-7 record. Modell had lost confidence in Rutigliano. There also was a sense among the front office and some key players that the team needed a different personality as a head coach. Rutigliano was considered more of "players' coach," not especially strict.

But the real reason the Browns were losing was the lack of a quarterback. Brian Sipe had left Cleveland for the USFL after the 1983 season. Paul McDonald had taken his place, and he proved it was very hard to replace the popular and productive Sipe.

Modell also had been frustrated since the Browns lost the Red Right 88 playoff game after the 1980 season. The team lost in the playoffs again in 1982.

That's the background. The immediate trigger to fire Rutigliano in 1984 was a 12-9 loss in Cincinnati. Modell took those games very personally. The Bengals were owned by the family of former

Browns coach Paul Brown—the man fired by Modell after the 1962 season.

"We're going to make a change," said Modell. "I want to replace Sam with Marty."

From what Accorsi had watched in his brief time with the Browns, it was the right move.

* * *

When the team arrived back in Cleveland after the loss to the Bengals, Modell called Accorsi and Schottenheimer to ask them to meet him at his home.

When Schottenheimer answered the phone, he assumed Modell was firing him and everyone else. The team was 1-7. Rumors of Rutigliano's possible firing had been in the media for a few weeks. But Schottenheimer also knew an owner doesn't summon you to his home to dump you. He'd do that on the phone.

"I'm making a change," Modell told Schottenheimer at the meeting. "I'm going to name you head coach."

Schottenheimer had an idea that was coming.

"I'm going to give you a trial for the last eight weeks of the season," said Modell, "I'm naming you interim head coach and then I'll make a decision at the end of the year."

"Fine," said Schottenheimer. "I don't want the job."

"Why?" asked a stunned Modell.

Schottenheimer stared hard at the owner. There was a long silence.

"I'm not taking the job under those conditions," explained Schottenheimer. "Players don't respect interim coaches. If you want me to coach the team, then make me the coach. There has to be commitment. I want a 3-year contract. I want a public commitment that I'm going to be here next year, no matter what happens this season."

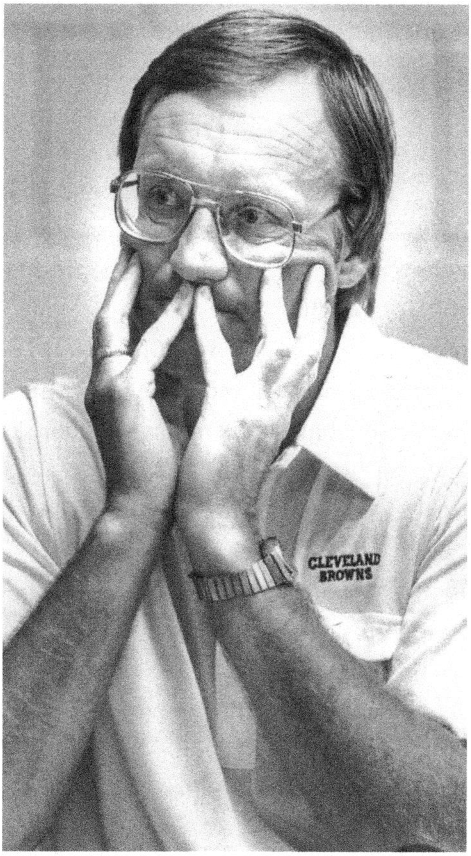

Marty Schottenheimer did everything with passion. Here, he ponders a reporter's question during a press conference in 1985. *Timothy Barmann / Plain Dealer*

For one of the few times in his life, Modell was speechless. Part of him thought Schottenheimer had lost his mind. How could this guy turn down a chance to be head coach of the Cleveland Browns—under any circumstances?

Modell finally told Schottenheimer to wait a few minutes. The owner asked Accorsi to join him in the kitchen.

"What do you think?" asked Modell.

"You better give him the job," said Accorsi. "I'm not coaching this team."

Accorsi was impressed by Schottenheimer's stance. He knew Schottenheimer was right. The vast majority of interim head coaches were destined to fail. They were desperate to get the job and would take it under any conditions—and the players knew that. It hurt their credibility.

"I had already been impressed by Marty," said Accorsi. "This just made me admire him even more. He was confident. He knew what he wanted and what it took to have a chance at being successful."

Modell and Accorsi left the kitchen and returned to Schottenheimer.

"Congratulations," said the owner. "You have a contract for the rest of this season plus two more years."

The Browns finished 4-4 under Schottenheimer. Accorsi thought it was a remarkable achievement. Recognizing the weakness at quarterback with Paul McDonald, Schottenheimer turned to a power running game with Mike Pruitt, Boyce Green and Earnest Byner.

Schottenheimer believed the team lacked toughness. He held practices outside in the snow . . . long practices. When players complained, he gave them the Schottenheimer Stare that shut them up in mid-sentence. This wasn't punishment. The Browns played games outside in the wind, cold and snows of November and December on shores of Lake Erie. The players should practice in lousy weather, too. His film sessions could be brutal on players who were seen not hustling. But the players also began to realize Schottenheimer was being critical for a reason. The team had problems and wasn't paying attention to details.

"Marty was a good teacher," said Kevin Byrne, the Browns'

former public relations director. “He also hired good teachers to be on his coaching staff. One of his strengths was to figure out what it would take to win that week’s game, then come up with a blueprint for the players to do it.”

Often, Schottenheimer highlighted three points to victory. He gave the players clear steps to reach those goals. He was selling his team on his “one play at time” philosophy. Pay attention to each individual play. What is your individual job on that particular play? That was what he’d ask players so they understood their jobs.

“Marty could have been a great teacher in almost any subject,” said Byrne. “He had the ability to break things down so they were easy to understand.”

In 1985, Accorsi found a way to acquire Bernie Kosar in the NFL’s supplemental draft. He signed veteran Gary Danielson to open the season at quarterback. Once again, Schottenheimer stayed with the ground game. Newly acquired Kevin Mack joined Byner as each rushed for 1,000 yards. This was designed to keep the pressure off Kosar in his rookie season. The Browns finished 8-8.

That set up the best run for the Browns since the 1960s.

The Browns made the playoffs in all four of Schottenheimer’s full seasons as head coach. His time in Cleveland has been unfairly cast as one of frustrations, losing in the playoffs to Denver twice—The Drive and The Fumble games.

“Marty and I hit it off,” said Accorsi. “As it turned out, I’ve had a closer relationship to him than any other coach in my career. I don’t think people fully appreciate the great job he did in Cleveland.”

BEYOND THE DRIVE AND THE FUMBLE: THE BROWNS OF THE LATE 1980S

When the Browns of the late 1980s are mentioned, two things come up:

The Drive . . .

The Fumble.

That's understandable, but also ridiculous.

I know the players from those teams agree with that assertion. Their good work from 1985 to 1989 with the coming of Bernie Kosar should not be written off as a pair of playoff losses that still torment some Browns fans.

Once, even I fell into the trap. I asked Kosar, "What was worse, The Drive or the Fumble?"

"Can't say," he explained. "They both sucked. But I felt worse for Earnest Byner (The Fumble). He's such a good man. I think about him every day. I admire how he handled all that."

Now we're on to something that comes closer to the heart of the Browns and the players from that era.

"Such a good man," said Kosar of Byner, who fumbled near the goal line in the 1987 AFC Championship Game.

But as I mention in this book's chapter about Kevin Mack and

Byner, even if Byner crossed the goal line for the TD—and the Browns kicked the extra point—the score would have been tied. Denver and John Elway would have been receiving the kickoff with 72 seconds left.

But I'm stopping right there.

Instead, I'm thinking about how Bernie Kosar and his family, along with Browns GM Ernie Accorsi, worked the 1985 Supplemental Draft so the quarterback from Youngstown could become a Cleveland Brown.

I'm thinking about how Kosar went to some Browns games as a kid. He had a Browns wastebasket in his room.

I'm thinking about how Kosar told me it was nice to be on a Super Bowl winning team in Dallas, "But my goal was to win a Super Bowl for Cleveland. It's why I wanted to play there in the first place."

I'm thinking about how Kevin Mack, Reggie Langhorne, Brian Brennan and many other players from that era have memories of how the old Stadium seemed to shake when the team was introduced before games. Their hearts pounded. Some of their eyes watered. They felt trickles of sweat running down their backs.

Something special was about to happen.

That's what it was like for the Browns players and their fans in the late 1980s.

No marketing department developed "the Dawgs." That identity was a product of the imagination of defensive backs Hanford Dixon and Frank Minnifield.

"It was something we did in practice," said Minnifield. "We used to say the quarterback was the cat and we were the dogs. The cat had no chance against us."

Woof . . . woof.

Bark . . . bark . . . BARK!

Minnifield and Dixon barking during training camp.

Then other members of the defense were barking, led by linebacker Eddie Johnson.

Then the fans heard . . . and they were barking.

Woof . . . woof.

Bark . . . bark . . . BARK!

"Here we go Brownies, here we go . . . WOOF . . . WOOF!'

Looks and sounds dumb, especially on the printed page.

Minnifield posted this on the Blanton Collier Foundation website:

> The Dawg Pound started during the 1985 Training Camp at Lakeland Community College in Kirtland, Ohio. Hanford and I started the idea of the pound to try to get more pressure on the quarterback. We had the idea of the quarterback being the cat, and the defensive line being the dog. Whenever the defense would get a regular sack or a coverage sack, the defensive linemen and linebackers would bark. This attitude carried into the stands at training camp, where fans started barking along with the players. We then put up the first 'Dawg Pound' banner in front of the bleachers before the first preseason game at the old Cleveland Stadium. The bleacher section had the cheapest seats in the stadium, and its fans were already known as the most vocal. They adopted their new identity whole-heartedly, wearing dog noses, dog masks, bone-shaped hats and other outlandish costumes.
>
> Woof . . . Woof. There you have it.
>
> Franky Minnifield

So that's right from the Dawg's mouth, or keyboard in this case.

In his book "Day of the Dawg," Dixon wrote about one day saying in the huddle, "Think of the quarterback like he's a cat, and you're a dog. The dog needs to catch the cat."

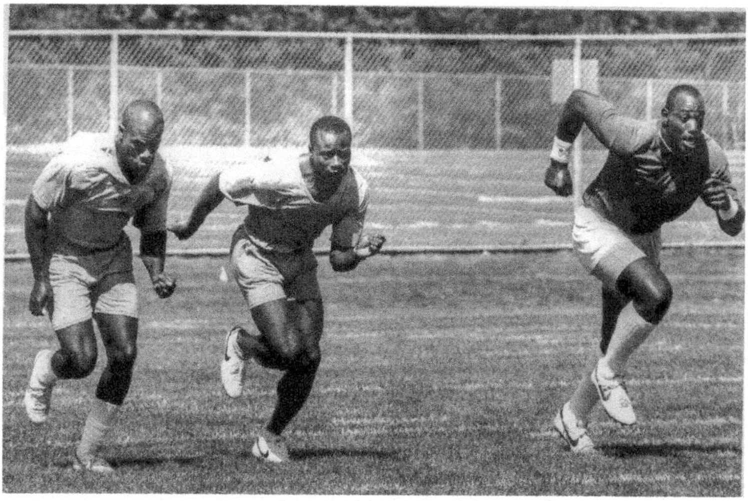

Hanford Dixon, Frank Minnifield and Ozzie Newsome at Browns Training Camp in 1986. *Marvin M. Greene / The Plain Dealer*

As the defense lined up for a play, Dixon said, "I let out a few barks . . . Before the next play, I let out a few more barks. Pretty soon, it was a matter of routine . . . it didn't take long for the fans at practice to start barking."

The stories basically match. The point is simple and profound.

It happened naturally.

Today, the marketers would say "organically." But I don't like the term for this reason—it's a marketing term. They want to "create things" that grow organically. But they want it to be their idea.

Minnifield and Dixon wanted to light a fire under their defense. Minnifield and Dixon saw themselves as underdogs—they loved the dog imagery—like their city and their fans. Dixon also wrote of a "front office administrator" who called him into the office one day.

"Hanford, all this stuff about dogs and barking is a distraction," said the administrator. "We're not the Cleveland Dogs. We're the Cleveland Browns. We don't have a logo on our helmets and we're not about to. And we already have a mascot."

He meant "Brownie," the elf-like figure.

"The fans like it," said Dixon, as he recounts in his book written with Randy Nyerges.

It showed how out-of-touch some people are in marketing departments and front offices. If it's not their idea, they don't like it.

Furthermore, telling two stubborn, emotionally driven athletes such as Dixon and Minnifield not to bark will make them howl with laughter.

And bark more.

And urge the fans to do the same.

Soon fans came to games in Dawg outfits and masks. They brought fake Dawg Bones and some of the real things—firing Milk-Bone dog treats at opposing players in front of the Dawg Pound in one of the end zones at the old Stadium.

"The Dawg Pound was created by Hanford and Minnifield," said Kevin Byrne. "The organization had nothing to do with it. And as they both told me through the years, they didn't get a penny for it."

Dixon and Minnifield brought some confidence . . . even cockiness . . . when they teamed up for the Browns in 1984.

* * *

It's usually the quarterback who drives the engine. It was GM Ernie Accorsi's decision to boldly trade for the supplemental draft rights to pick Kosar in 1985 that put the Browns on the right track.

"I remember Bernie's last year with (the University of) Miami," said Accorsi. "They had him miked-up on the field. (Coach) Jimmy Johnson was telling him to run the ball and then they'd kick a field goal. Bernie said, 'I'm going for the touchdown.' It was very direct, no baloney. Not a phony bone in his body. That's what I wanted for our quarterback."

And yes, Kosar threw for a touchdown on that next play.

The remarkable part of the "Kosar to Cleveland" story is that it worked.

Kosar put himself in a boiling pot of hometown pressure. He immediately became the highest paid player on the team and one of the highest paid in the NFL in 1985. It would have been easy for his teammates to resent him. He was 21 and had played only two years in college during an era when players stayed four years in school.

But Kosar did more than graduate ahead of schedule at Miami with his degree in finance. He was taking what amounted to graduate courses in quarterbacking. The Hurricanes had an assistant named Earl Morrall, who played 21 years in the NFL. He tutored Kosar.

Miami head coach Howard Schnellenberger is quoted in a 1984 Sports Illustrated story: "Nine out of 10 times, he threw to the right man. That's not 75 percent, that's 90 percent. And that is amazing."

Schnellenberger also said Kosar "successfully" changed plays all but 8% of the time when he was blitzed.

This was no ordinary kid quarterback coming to Cleveland, and Accorsi knew it. Accorsi remembered working for the old Baltimore Colts when he was a young man, and watching Johnny Unitas in practice. He didn't think the veteran quarterback had a very strong arm.

A veteran scout asked him, "Does he move the ball down the field?"

"Yes, he does," said Accorsi.

The lesson stayed with him. It's why Kosar's unorthodox throwing style and his lack of elite arm strength never worried Accorsi.

He had his Unitas. He even gave Kosar No. 19—the number Unitas wore in Baltimore.

* * *

Kosar signed a 5-year, $5 million deal with the Browns, including a $1 million signing bonus. Because he went into the supplemental draft, held months after the regular draft, there were no minicamps for Kosar as a rookie in 1985.

"I didn't know a single play (with the Browns)," he said. "I didn't know the terminology. I had to get the Browns to be a winning team and get to the playoffs. I didn't want to be the weak link."

Kosar struggled in the preseason. Veteran Gary Danielson had been acquired by Accorsi to start at quarterback, to keep the pressure off Kosar.

But Kosar felt the pressure anyway.

"I was suddenly with men," he said. "I was 21 and I'm looking Ozzie Newsome in the eye in the huddle. I was in the locker room with guys like Clay Matthews. I was the highest paid rookie ever."

Kosar paused, thinking back.

"I didn't even know the snap counts," he said. "I was taking a crash course to learn everything fast . . . and I was supposed to be the savior? That's why I was grateful the great Ernie Accorsi was wise enough to bring in Gary Danielson. He was a huge help to me."

Danielson started the first five games, then broke his ankle during the New England game. Kosar finished up that game and the Browns won, 24-20. The next week, he went to Houston and won his first start, 21-6.

The Browns finished 8-8 that season. But it was clear they had found a quarterback.

* * *

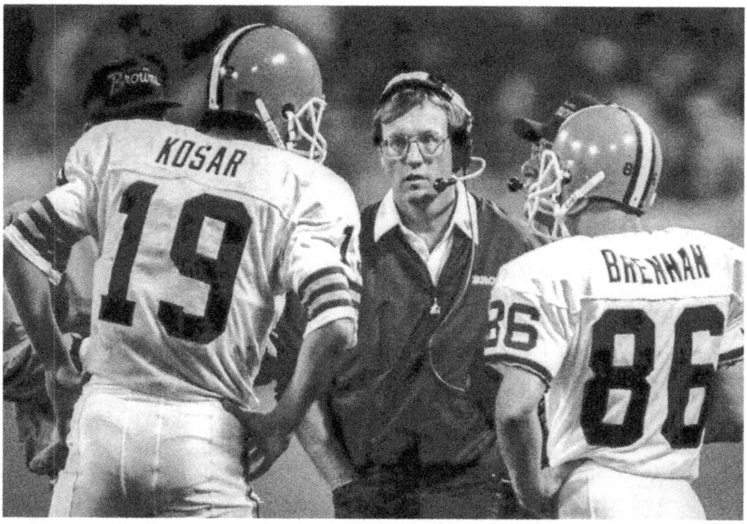

Bernie Kosar and Brian Brennan discuss strategy on the sideline with Marty Schottenheimer in 1986. *Richard T. Conway / The Plain Dealer*

In Kosar's second season, Lindy Infante was hired as offensive coordinator. Coach Marty Schottenheimer moved Joe Pendry from offensive coordinator to running backs coach. The Browns went from a power-run offense with Kevin Mack and Earnest Byner to one powered by the passing and wits of Kosar.

Today, many people assume Infante and Kosar were immediately a perfect match. Infante had five years of experience calling plays in the NFL.

"It took a while," said Accorsi, who then told a story of the first meeting in 1986 before training camp opened.

"What do you think of Kosar?" owner Art Modell asked Infante.

"I don't think we can win with him," said Infante. "He's not mobile . . . "

Before Infante could finish the rest of his sentence, Modell said, "Go get Marty"—head coach Marty Schottenheimer.

Accorsi left the room to get the coach.

As Accorsi and Schottenheimer walked together to meet Modell and Infante, "Marty was seething," according to Accorsi.

Modell was shocked. He had paid what was considered an outrageous amount of money and draft capital to obtain and sign Kosar.

Schottenheimer walked into the room. Before anyone said anything, Schottenheimer roared, "WE WILL WIN WITH HIM!"

The Kosar discussion was over.

"And we did win with Bernie," said Accorsi. "As Lindy got to know him and work with him, Lindy saw the same things in Bernie the rest of us did."

Accorsi also considered bringing Infante to Cleveland "a big prize. We all wanted Lindy. Other teams wanted him, too."

The offense opened up. The Browns not only won, they were fun to watch.

"We suddenly went 4-wide (on some plays)," recalled receiver Reggie Langhorne, meaning four receivers going out for passes.

The offense now belonged to Kosar. He changed plays at the line of scrimmage, much like he did at Miami. And the quarterback and coordinator became one, much like Kosar had with his key coaches at Miami. Kosar was excited because he could throw more, "and it made our offense less predictable."

Meanwhile, Infante dismissed Kosar's lack of mobility as "overdone and overrated" in a press conference. Brian Brennan remembered how Kosar threw the ball "at just the right time," and how it was "so catchable."

Kosar not only enjoyed throwing passes to receivers Webster Slaughter, Langhorne and Brennan, he made Byner a receiving weapon coming out of the backfield. And he had future Hall of Famer Ozzie Newsome at tight end.

"We could score," said Langhorne. "When we were on our game, no one was like us."

Here's what Sports Illustrated's Rick Telander wrote about Kosar in 1988: "(He's) a 24-year-old gawk of a quarterback, the kid with an accountant's body and altar boy's face."

Telander also wrote this:

"(He) has thrown underhanded passes. In fact, he has thrown from almost every arm angle there is—always with remarkable accuracy—as if his right arm were a minute hand on a precision Swiss clock that has every number on its face but high noon."

In 1986 working with Infante, Kosar threw 17 TD passes compared to 10 interceptions, completing 58% of his passes. At one point, he threw 171 passes without an interception. Those numbers look modest by today's pass-obsessed standards, but it was a different world back then.

In 1987, Kosar had 22 TD passes compared to nine interceptions, completing 62% of his throws. More importantly, the Browns were 12-4 and 10-5 in those two seasons.

After the 1987 season, Infante left to become the head coach of the Packers, where he was rewarded with a 5-year contract. Accorsi recalls this conversation:

"I have to tell you, I was dead wrong about Bernie," said Infante.

"Lindy, part of the reason you were wrong was you," said Accorsi. "You had a lot to do with being wrong. You did such a great job with him, you made yourself wrong. People couldn't stop us."

There is a lesson here. Infante was willing to open his mind to Kosar. Rather than trying to prove he was right, he recognized that his job was to make the offense work with the quarterback he had.

And Infante did just that.

* * *

I refuse to spend much time discussing The Drive and The Fumble in this book. If you want to look at those events in detail, they each received a separate chapter in my book, "Things I Learned From Watching The Browns."

I'm going to take the Kosar approach.

"The Browns of the 1980s were like family to me," said the quarterback. "It was before free agency. We stayed together. After I had some problems in my life, guys like Dan Fike, Reggie Langhorne and Tim Manoa called right away. So did lots of others."

Kosar talked about the "special relationship" the team had with fans, the city and each other. It's why he rarely turns down autograph requests.

"How hard is it to take 20 seconds and sign your name?" he said. "It means a lot to me that fans still care. It's easy to sign and talk a little with them."

Fans will recall the "Bernie Bernie" song, sung to the tune of "Louie Louie." They'll talk about The Drive and The Fumble, but then they'll thank Kosar for the memories . . . the overall experience of that era. Those teams made Sunday games must watch occasions—be it in person or on television.

"That team captivated the town," recalled Accorsi. "There were so many great performances. It was magical. And that 1986 playoff game . . ."

Accorsi was talking about the come-from-behind playoff victory over the Jets . . . yes, he was talking about a playoff win!

In 1986, "it was like we exploded," said receiver Reggie Langhorne. He meant the offense designed by Infante and engineered by Kosar. The Browns finished 12-4. Think about that: from 5-11 to 12-4 and a playoff victory in two years.

The Browns offense went from being ranked No. 23 in scoring in 1985 to No. 5 in 1986.

"We were fun to watch," said Langhorne. "And it was a lot of fun to play in that offense."

You can win some money in a bet with Browns fans knowing

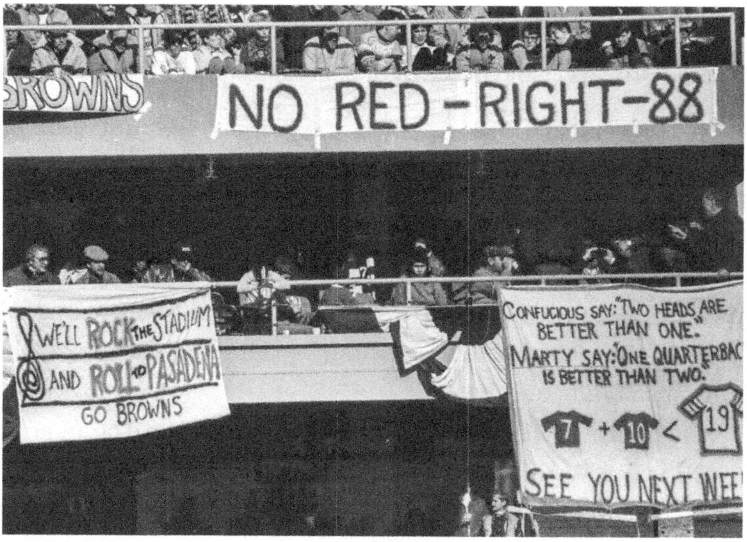

Fans on the edge of their seats on Jan. 3, 1987. "Red Right 88" was still a recent painful memory when the Browns fans suffered "The Drive" and "The Fumble." But those teams deserve to be remembered for so much more than those two moments. *Richard T. Conway / The Plain Dealer*

the answer to this question: In 1986, what Browns receiver led the team in receptions and TD catches?

Most fans would mention Webster Slaughter or Langhorne. Or perhaps, Byner, who was such a pass-catching weapon for Kosar out of the backfield.

It was Brian Brennan, 55 receptions and 6 TD catches.

"Brian had a lot of confidence," said Kevin Byrne. "He didn't care he was 5-foot-10 or whatever. His approach was, 'Just keep throwing me the ball, I'll show you how good I am . . . if you really want to win, throw me the ball.' "

Byrne saw much the same attitude from Byner, the 10th round draft choice: "Earnest's thought process was, 'You have all these fast, sleek guys—if you want to get the ball down the field, give me the ball.' "

* * *

The Browns also had the right coaching staff.

"Marty was at top of his game," said Accorsi. "Infante was a great offensive coordinator. Howard Mudd was as good an offensive line coach as you'd find in the NFL. There was a special relationship between the front office, coaches and players that year."

Langhorne talked about how "Marty could get inside your head and make you believe in yourself. He had a way of making you want to do something for him, because you knew he really did care about you."

Langhorne vividly remembers how he was told he'd be a starter.

"It was a Wednesday," he said. "Marty walked up to me. He stopped and just stared. Didn't say anything. He just stared, like he was reading me."

Then what?

"I was thinking, 'What is he looking at me for?'" said Langhorne.

Then what?

"Lang," said Schottenheimer. "Are you ready to start?"

"Yeah!" said Langhorne.

"You work with the first team this week," said Schottenheimer.

That was it, no lecture. Just the straight scoop from the coach.

"Marty was perfect for those teams," said Byrne. "He didn't need a lot of personal attention. He was glad to let the players have it. He was a former player, he understood that it was his job to teach and coach—not take credit for what went right. But he was there to protect his players in front of the media when things went wrong. Now, the players knew when it came time for practice and game preparation, there was no screwing around when Marty was in charge."

Byrne remembers watching practices when Kosar made some bad throws.

"Hey Bernie," Schottenheimer would yell. "If you do that on Sunday, we'll lose. Got that?"

Or Schottenheimer would say to a defensive back such as Minnifield: "Hey Frank, you can't let your guy turn his steps in that direction because the safety won't be there. That's going to be YOUR fault. Quit screwing around, do it right."

"Guys respected Marty because he played in the NFL," said Brennan. "He also was a student of the game. He appreciated hard work and knowing your responsibilities. He made things clear, and the players appreciated that."

* * *

Then there was Kosar.

"Bernie played without fear," said Kevin Byrne. "Bernie poured so much of himself into the games. When it was over—win or lose—he was exhausted. Sometimes when he talked to the media after games, his hands would shake. He pushed his mind and body to the extreme."

Kosar played like a man who believed he was more than a quarterback. He was carrying the hopes and dreams of his family and Browns fans everywhere on his thin shoulders.

"Bernie got it, the entire thing about being a quarterback," said Byrne. "You didn't have to tell Bernie to go over to Byner after he fumbled—or up to another player after he made a mistake. Bernie did it right away. He knew how important he was to his teammates."

Langhorne said it was challenging for Kosar "to try to keep us all happy."

He meant receivers Webster Slaughter, Brennan and himself. He meant Ozzie Newsome at tight end. He meant running backs Kevin Mack and Byner.

"Bernie had a way of keeping you involved," said Langhorne.

"When a play wasn't designed for you, he sometimes would pull you aside and say, 'Don't sleep on me. If the coverage goes a certain way, I'm going to take a shot (downfield) with you.' He made you feel important—and if the coverage broke a certain way, he would throw it to you."

* * *

The Browns and their fans had four wonderful years with Kosar and Schottenheimer.

"The players believed in Marty and Bernie," said Byrne. "Unfortunately, John Elway kept us from making three Super Bowls."

Byrne was talking about 1986 and 1987 when Schottenheimer was coach, and being knocked out of the playoffs after the 1989 season under Bud Carson.

It was much like the Cavs, who kept running into Michael Jordan and the Chicago Bulls. Five times, they were knocked out of the playoffs by a Jordan-led team. Not every year would they have gone to the NBA Finals, but it could have happened at least in a few of those seasons.

Elway was the Michael Jordan of quarterbacks during several of those seasons.

"I still talk to John Elway," said Kosar. "But we never talk about The Drive or The Fumble. It's too painful for me. We talk about some of the guys we played with, and even some of the plays in certain games. But not The Drive or The Fumble."

Kosar knows, there are times in life when you say, "It wasn't perfect, but it was good. It was really a good time."

MACK & BYNER

It's almost as if they are the same person, one name.

Mack & Byner.

At least, that's how some Browns fans remember them.

Whenever the Browns have two good running backs, some fans reach back to the past and wonder, "Can they be like Mack & Byner?"

Two running backs melting into one powerhouse force in the backfield.

Mack & Byner.

Two guys from small Southern towns who came to Cleveland with very little hype.

Mack & Byner.

"They were the guys who helped make life much easier for Bernie (Kosar) when he was a rookie," said Ernie Accorsi. He was the general manager who added Mack and Kosar in different supplemental drafts.

Kevin Mack & Earnest Byner.

Just saying those names should make Browns fans of a certain age smile. Hearing their stories is inspiring.

Until writing this book, I forgot Mack & Byner didn't come into the NFL together—although they were both in the same draft class of 1984.

The Browns picked Byner in the 10th round, No. 280 overall. He played at East Carolina, where he had good but not great stats as a running back.

"You didn't hear much about Earnest before that draft," recalled Ernie Accorsi. "I had joined the Browns, but it was (former player personnel director) Bill Davis who picked Byner."

But early in training camp, even before the 1984 preseason games began, Ozzie Newsome came up to Accorsi.

"Byner is going to be special," Newsome told Accorsi.

That led Accorsi to pay close attention to Byner.

"He didn't have great speed," said Accorsi. "But we had this thing called the 'Reaction Box' that was invented by the Dallas Cowboys."

It's hard to explain, but it was a device set up to measure a player's ability to change direction and have a quick first few steps.

"Earnest blew up the box!" recalled Accorsi, his voice rising. "I mean, blew it up. Forget his time in the 40 (yard dash). He was powerful and that change of direction . . . that's what made him special."

Kevin Byrne recalled a conversation he had in 1984 with Keith Rowen, the team's running backs coach.

"I like that 10th rounder," Rowen said. "They're really hard to tackle, those bow-legged guys. They have a wide base and they're just hard to knock down. That guy Byner has a feel for it. He's not the fastest guy in the world, but he's going to play."

The 1984 Browns were a mess. Brian Sipe had left for the New Jersey Generals of the USFL. Paul McDonald was overmatched as the starting quarterback. Coach Sam Rutigliano was starting Mike Pruitt and Boyce Green in the backfield. They combined to average 3.2 yards per carry.

Byner did start three games and played in all 16. He rushed for 426 yards, 5.9 per carry. Rutigliano was fired at midseason after a

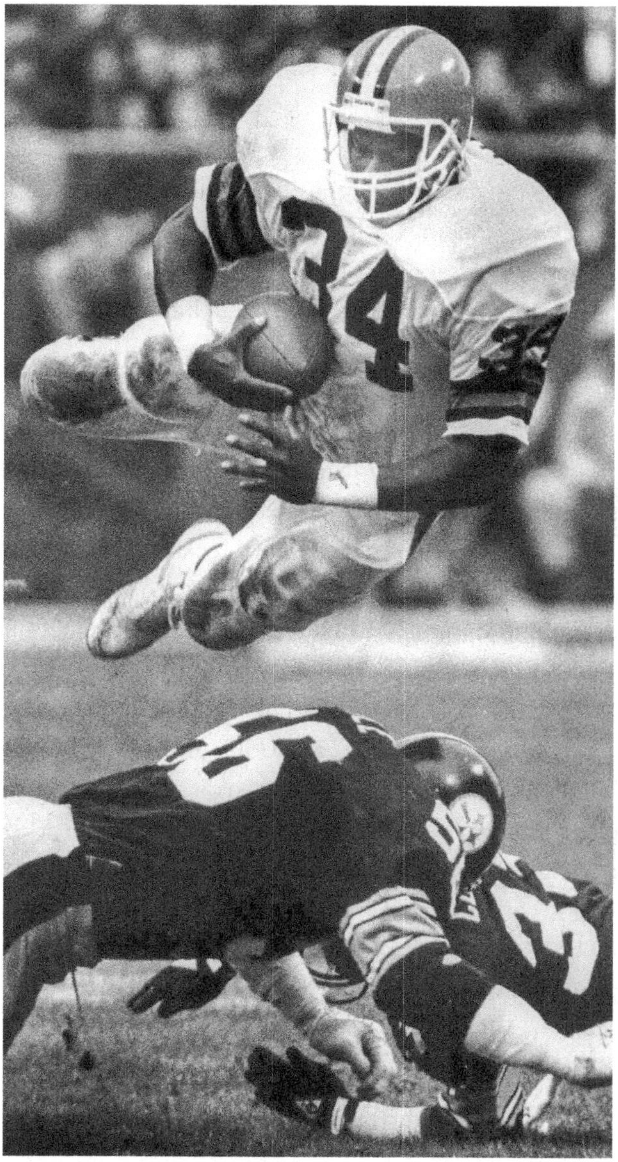

Kevin Mack leaps over the Steelers in 1988. He and Earnest Byner were a powerhouse running duo that made Bernie Kosar's job easier. *Richard T. Conway / The Plain Dealer*

1-7 start. Marty Schottenheimer took over as head coach, and he was a Byner fan.

* * *

While Byner was catching the attention of the Browns coaching staff, Mack was playing for the Los Angeles Express of the USFL.

"I never started at Clemson until my senior year," he said. "I didn't get a lot of recognition. It's hard to believe, but I was a full-back at a buck-87."

A 187-pound fullback?

"That's right," said Mack. "My coach at Clemson (Danny Ford) said he thought I could at least get an NFL tryout if I didn't get drafted."

In his senior season at Clemson, Mack ran for 862 yards, an average of 5.7 per carry. Good stats on a 9-1-1 team that was on NCAA probation but still ranked in the top 10 in most polls. He was picked in the USFL draft, held in January of 1984.

"It wasn't like now when guys know all about their draft status when in college," said Mack. "The USFL offered me some money much like the NFL was paying, so I took it. I didn't even know if I would get drafted by the NFL. I didn't wait to find out."

Mack was a part-time player for the Express, rushing for 330 yards on 73 carries. He was good enough to remain with the team, but the USFL and the Express were bleeding money. Players were being cut to slash the payroll.

That included Mack.

"I didn't know what I was going to do next," said Mack. "I didn't know if I was good enough to play in the NFL."

Accorsi had scouted Mack at Clemson. He saw a fast fullback who could add weight.

"I don't know if he would have been taken in the first round, but he'd have been drafted (in 1984)," said Accorsi. "I know, I would have drafted him at some point."

The NFL held a supplemental draft for teams to pick up the rights to USFL and Canadian Football League players on June 5, 1984. Accorsi selected Mack with the No. 11 pick overall. He also added linebacker Mike Johnson and Gerald "Ice Cube" McNeil.

The moment Accorsi saw that Mack had been cut, he was on the phone with the fullback's agent.

Mack didn't know about the supplemental draft the year before. He had no idea he had been picked by the Browns. He just knew his agent now told him to immediately get on a plane to Cleveland.

"I came to Cleveland in February," he said. "I had never been there before. I knew no one. I got off the plane wearing a summer jacket and froze my butt off."

He met with the Browns, signing a contract for "about $175,000." The only part guaranteed was a signing bonus for "about $35,000."

* * *

"I remember they had eight running backs in camp," said Mack, who mentioned Boyce Green, Mike Pruitt, Johnny Davis and Byner. "I knew Mike Pruitt had been really good. I was worried about making the team. I wasn't sure what they wanted me to do."

Mack quickly connected with Byner and began following him around.

"One day Earnest said we could start in the backfield," said Mack. "He could see how it could happen. We worked out at the same time. We pushed each other."

Byner's vision was Mack at fullback, himself at halfback. Byner knew Marty Schottenheimer wanted a punishing running game and the coach wasn't happy with his 1984 starters.

"When I first met Marty, I thought he was tough and kind of mean," said Mack. "I was never an overly confident guy on the field. I was always wondering, 'Did I do that right?'"

Mack said veterans had told him to beware when someone

knocks on your door and asks you to follow him with your playbook.

"That means it's over," said Mack. "So I didn't stay in my room that much. If they knocked, I didn't want them to find me."

Byner kept reassuring Mack that things would work out, but doubts haunted him.

"Kevin was a quiet kid from a small Southern town," said Accorsi. "We knew how good he was. But he didn't know it."

Mack was from Kings Mountain, N.C. It's about 30 miles west of Charlotte and was a town of about 8,000 when Mack was growing up. Byner was from Milledgeville, Georgia. So the two young men had rural Southern roots and common dreams of starting for the Browns.

"We had a scrimmage against Buffalo," recalled Mack. "I remember being on the bus, wondering if I would make the team. Then before the scrimmage started, I was nervous. It was one of the most nerve-wracking times I remember."

Schottenheimer spotted it. The coach walked over to Mack.

"Look, calm down and relax," Schottenheimer said. "You are better than 90% of the guys on the field."

Mack looked at the coach in a moment of disbelief.

"Just go out there, play ball and have fun," said Schottenheimer.

"That changed everything for me," said Mack. "It meant so much to know he had that confidence in me. He really thought I was better than a lot of those guys out there."

How did Mack find out he made the team?

"No one actually told me," he said. "When they took the team picture and I was still there, then I knew . . . "

* * *

Mack & Byner.

For Schottenheimer and the Browns, the 1985 season was

Earnest Byner in 1988. "Byner is going to be special," Ozzie Newsome said during Byner's first training camp in 1984. *Nancy Stone / The Plain Dealer*

the start of one of the most fun and successful periods since the Browns' glory days of the 1940s, 1950s and 1960s.

The Browns opened with Mack and Byner in the backfield. Accorsi had added Bernie Kosar in the 1985 Supplemental Draft. Veteran Gary Danielson started the first six games, then was injured.

"We had to protect Kosar," said Accorsi. "When I traded for Danielson, I wanted him to start. I didn't want to immediately start Bernie. Nor did I want to play Paul McDonald. I wanted a strong running game, no matter who was the quarterback."

The Browns were determined to run the ball and keep the pressure off Kosar. Mack and Byner each had 1,000-yard rushing seasons.

"We weren't going to beat people by trying to throw for 350 yards," said Accorsi. "Not with Bernie as a rookie. We played an old-fashioned two-backs set and pounded the ball. Those guys were perfect for each other."

* * *

The Fumble.

Too many have attached those two words next to the name of Earnest Byner.

It happened in the 1987 AFC Championship Game. The Browns were playing at Denver. Memory is not always reliable. Too many Browns fans believe if Byner had hung on to the football—and not lost a fumble on the Denver 2-yard line—the Browns would have beat the Broncos and gone to the Super Bowl.

One problem with all that. It's wrong.

The Browns were losing 38-31 and had driven 72 yards in seven plays late in the game.

Remember, the score was 38-31.

There was 1:12 left on the clock. Byner had what he thought was an open lane to the end zone. But on the 2-yard-line, he was hit from the side and fumbled.

Denver recovered.

Ballgame. The Broncos took a 2-point safety with 8 seconds left to make the final score 38-33.

But let's suppose Byner had scored that touchdown. And the extra point was good. The score would have been 38-38.

The score would have been tied with a minute left and the Browns kicking the ball to Denver and quarterback John Elway. The Browns hadn't stopped the Broncos all day. Denver had 412 yards on offense. They averaged 20 yards per pass reception. And Elway was playing at home.

At best, the regulation game would have ended at 38-38. Then there would have been a coin flip to see what team received the ball for the overtime period.

Byner carried the ball 15 times for 67 yards in that game, including a rushing touchdown. He was Cleveland's leading receiver, catching seven passes for 120 yards and another touchdown. He had the Browns' longest run (16 yards) and longest reception (53 yards) in the game. Only Kosar (26-of-41 passing, 356 yards and three TD passes) had a better day for Cleveland on offense.

That's why Kosar and Newsome came up to a distraught Byner on the sidelines and told him the team would not have been in this position without him.

"I always appreciated that," Byner told me in 2010. "Carl ("Big Daddy") Hairston came up to me on the flight home after the game. I started to apologize. He put his big hand on my shoulder and said I had nothing to be sorry for. I was the reason we were even in the game until the end."

* * *

The most revealing part of the story happened after the game. Public relations director Kevin Byrne approached Byner in the locker room.

"I felt so bad for him," said Byrne. "It's one thing to fail. It's another thing to fail in public and then have to explain it to the media. Bernie and Earnest were the ones bringing us back in that game. And then the fumble . . . "

Byrne told Byner, "You're going to have to talk about this to the media."

"I don't know what to say," said Byner.

Byrne tried to prepare Byner with questions likely to be asked: What did he remember from the play? What was the play? Did he see the guy who hit him?

They agreed to wait 10 minutes, then Byner faced the media.

"The interview room in Denver was like a concrete bunker," said Byrne. "It could only hold about 30 media people at a time."

There were about 250 media people at the game.

Byner did one wave of questions . . . then another wave . . . and another. He offered no excuses, the fumble was his fault. He just didn't see the tackler coming. He thought he'd get into the end zone. Then the ball was gone. It happened so fast.

Then this question.

"Earnest, does it bother you that you're going to become known as the Bill Buckner of football?" asked Steve Serby of the New York Post.

Byner looked at Byrne, confused.

"I guess not," said Byner. "I don't know who Bill Buckner is."

With that, Byrne ended the press conference.

"I always thought it was a great line," said Byrne. "It was genuine. Earnest didn't know about Bill Buckner."

In Game 6 of the 1986 World Series, Buckner, playing first base for Boston, had a ball roll through his legs to cost the Red Sox a possible chance to win.

* * *

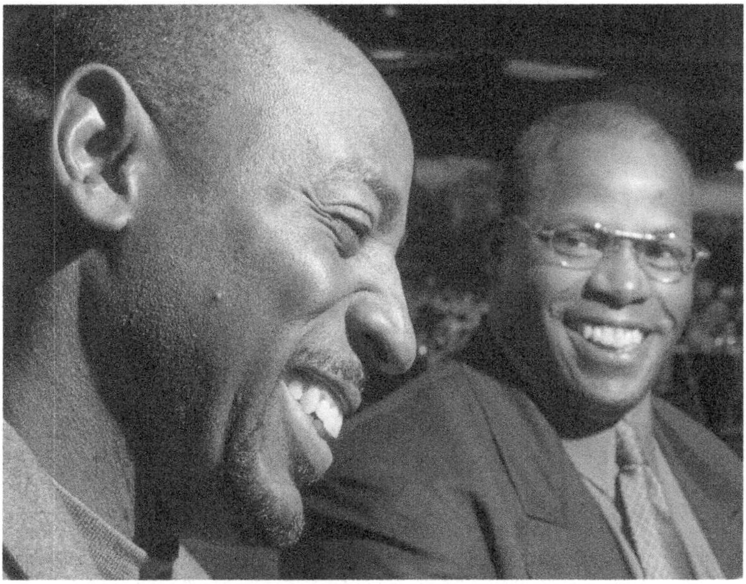

Earnest Byner, left, and Kevin Mack enjoy a light moment before a banquet at Brown Stadium in 2003. Both had difficulties during their careers, but both look back fondly. *Bill Kennedy / The Plain Dealer*

After losing to Denver on The Drive in the 1986 playoffs, followed by The Fumble in the 1987 playoffs, the team and Byner were shell-shocked.

The 1988 season would see the Browns finish 10-6 as they went through four different quarterbacks due to injuries. Byner had one of his worst NFL seasons, averaging only 3.7 yards per carry. Schottenheimer was beginning to clash with owner Art Modell.

"Those two losses back-to-back to Denver took so much out of us emotionally," said Byrne.

In a 1988 playoff loss to Houston, Byner was flagged for a pair of personal fouls.

After the season, after Schottenheimer left, Accorsi made what he knew was probably a bad deal, sending Byner to Washington for a marginal player, Mike Oliphant.

"I just thought Byner needed a fresh start," said Accorsi.

Byner was only 27 when he began playing for Washington coach Joe Gibbs, a man who loved the running game. From 1990 to 1992, Byner rushed for 1,219 yards, 1,048 yards and 998 yards. He made two Pro Bowls and played on a Super Bowl winning team.

He played 14 years in the NFL and is a borderline Hall of Fame player.

"I never ran away from The Fumble," he told me in 2010. "I wish I had a nickel for every time I saw it on TV. I even saw it on a Cavs playoff game broadcast."

When Byner returned to the Browns in 1994, he explained, "The fans treated me like a hero. They have always done that. We talk about The Fumble when I speak to groups. It's part of our shared legacy. We can learn how not to be stuck in bitterness and anger . . . dealing with it has made me a better person."

* * *

Kevin Mack also had his trials in his later years with the Browns.

He was arrested in 1989 on drug charges. Making it worse, his arrest was caught on television by a news reporter. Mack was eventually suspended by the NFL for four games and served 34 days of a six-month jail sentence.

"I let a lot of people down," said Mack. "I had to answer for what I did. You can't just ask for forgiveness; you also have to put in the work to correct it."

Mack indeed bounced back. He played for the Browns until he was cut by Bill Belichick in 1993. Like most running backs, Mack dealt with several painful injuries during his career. After coaching at Texas Southern, he returned to Cleveland and has spent the last 14 years working for the Browns, mostly in their alumni relations department.

Mack still appreciates how the Browns gave him a chance in

the NFL. They stuck with him during his 1989 arrest, then later brought him on board as part of the organization.

"Then there's the fans," he said. "They've embraced me. It means so much. I never imagined things could work out so well."

ONE OF US: BERNIE KOSAR

It began with Bernie Kosar.

Younger Browns fans sometimes wonder why there is so much reverence for a former Browns quarterback who never led the team to the Super Bowl, much less won one.

But to focus on the lack of a championship is to miss the real story.

That's the same mistake many people make when assessing the past by looking through the windshield of today rather than the rearview mirror of history.

Before Bernie Kosar arrived in 1985, the Browns had been to the playoffs only twice in the previous 12 years—losing both times. They had not won a playoff game since 1969.

But the troubles in Cleveland were more than the football team losing.

Consider this from a Sports Illustrated story of Aug. 25, 1985, before Kosar played his first regular season game with the Browns:

> Things are not always so idyllic in Cleveland, as you may know. Indeed, a case can be made that things are never idyllic in Cleveland. We are talking about a town that a Miami reporter says escaped being the most boring city in the NFL only because they let Indianapolis in. But stop it. The Mistake on the

Bernie Kosar, just three years out of high school, dons a Browns jersey after signing with the team in 1985. "I can make a difference," he said. *C.H. Pete Copeland / The Plain Dealer*

Lake. Stop it. A place where the river caught on fire. Stop it. A city that has the Indians. Stop it. Those were the bad old days B.B.—Before Bernie.

Kosar was aware of all of this because he was one of us. Still is. Grew up in Youngstown a Browns fan. Went to some games as a kid. Dreamed of one day wearing an orange helmet in the NFL.

"When I came to the Browns, our area was still the butt of national jokes," said Kosar. "The Cuyahoga River caught on fire. The city was bankrupt. The unemployment. In Miami, I heard all that. I shrugged it off, but it bothered me."

Kosar knew the Browns having a winning team wouldn't change the social and economic problems, but it would be an emotional lift for the city.

"I kept thinking I could go back there and do something about all the negative stuff," said Kosar. "I could help my family have security, and I could play for my favorite team. This was a childhood dream and I could make people happy who loved the Browns."

Kosar paused.

"I can make a difference," he said. "That's what I was thinking about coming home to the Browns."

And Kosar didn't simply wait for the Browns to draft him, he found a way to make it happen.

As Browns fans from that era love to say, "He picked us."

* * *

"Do you realize when the Browns drafted me, I was only three years out of (Youngstown) Boardman (High)?" said Kosar.

The year was 1985. Kosar, along with his advisors and former Browns GM Ernie Accorsi, had found an unprecedented road to Cleveland.

"I was only 21," said Kosar. "I had just finished my second season at the U."

Kosar was talking about the University of Miami, where he led the Hurricanes to a national title in 1983.

"I loved being at the U," said Kosar. "I was always slow and skinny. I didn't anticipate being a pro player. The goal was to get a degree. My father had me taking advanced placement courses in high school so I could get college credits. That's what it was about in the beginning."

Kosar didn't play as a freshman. He was red-shirted behind Jim Kelly, a future Hall of Famer. The next two seasons, Kosar beat out Vinny Testaverde and became a star.

"This was when the NFL had a rule against drafting players unless they were seniors," said Accorsi. "But there also was a little known part of the rule. A player could be eligible for the draft if he graduated."

Kosar joked, "I was one of the few guys who regularly attended class."

He didn't just go to class, he did the work. He was studying finance and economics. He was taking extra courses in the summer.

"I was cranking through 18 (credit) hours a semester and playing football," said Kosar. "I love math. I could do it in my head. I heard what my teachers told me and I had the ability to remember it."

When the 1984 college football season ended, Kosar had a plan for 1985. Not the NFL, but staying at Miami. He'd graduate, then go for his master's degree. He was named an Academic All-American with a 3.27 GPA in his dual major of Economics and Finance.

"We were going to be loaded," he said. "I could see us winning national titles in 1985 and 1986 if I stayed. My thinking was, 'These are my brothers. This is my calling.' Back then, no one left early for the NFL. It wasn't even discussed."

* * *

In Cleveland, Accorsi had been hired as an assistant to Browns owner Art Modell on March 5, 1984. Coach Sam Rutigliano was running the team, assisted by Bill Davis.

"I had very little say in personnel," said Accorsi. "But I told Art and everyone else there that we weren't going to win with Paul McDonald at quarterback."

Modell, Accorsi said, was enamored with Doug Flutie, a star at Boston College who upset Kosar's Miami team.

"Bernie's the guy I want," Accorsi told Modell.

Accorsi had scouted Kosar. He knew the quarterback had piled up college credits at a remarkable rate.

He began plotting to bring Kosar to Cleveland, using the graduating early loophole.

"My father had been picking my college classes," said Kosar. "After the season, my father had it laid out for me to take 18 credits in the spring, six more in the summer. Then I could graduate."

His parents had become aware of the early entry draft rule.

"I wasn't very receptive to it," said Kosar. "I wasn't even sure if the class I needed to graduate would be available in the summer."

But something else was happening.

"My family worked at U.S. Steel," said Kosar. "For so many years, we were laborers and it was a great job. But the mills started closing down in the 1970s. The jobs disappeared. I saw that as a little boy."

And Kosar knew what it meant.

If he turned pro, there would be money. Millions. It would be a game changer for his family.

"I was wrestling with the feeling of responsibility," said Kosar. "I was thinking that going back to The U, we'd win the national title. I'd probably win the Heisman Trophy. But was I being selfish?"

He had several meetings with his family and others. Finally, Kosar decided.

"I'd like to play for the Browns," he told his father. "That's what it would take to get me out of Miami."

* * *

Bernie Kosar laughs and waves to fans as he leaves the field after a Browns win in 1987. *Curt Chandler / The Plain Dealer*

"I remember some of the discussions about Bernie before the draft," said Kevin Byrne, the former Browns public relations director. "We heard from Miami how Vinny (Testaverde) looks like a stallion and plays like a stallion, but the gawky guy (Kosar) beat him out. All Bernie does is complete passes.' "

Byrne said Accorsi was a believer in boldly trying to acquire a quarterback.

"It was like Ozzie Newsome once told me," said Byrne. "There are two kinds of teams in the NFL. Those with a quarterback and those who don't have a quarterback. If you don't have one, you are lost in the desert."

The Brian Sipe Era had ended after the 1983 season. Paul McDonald was the only quarterback of note on the roster. In 1984, he had thrown 23 interceptions compared to only 14 TD passes. He completed 55% of his passes and was sacked 53 times. The Browns were 5-11.

"We had the sixth pick in the regular draft (in 1985)," said Accorsi. "I had been in touch with Dr. John Geletka. He was Ber-

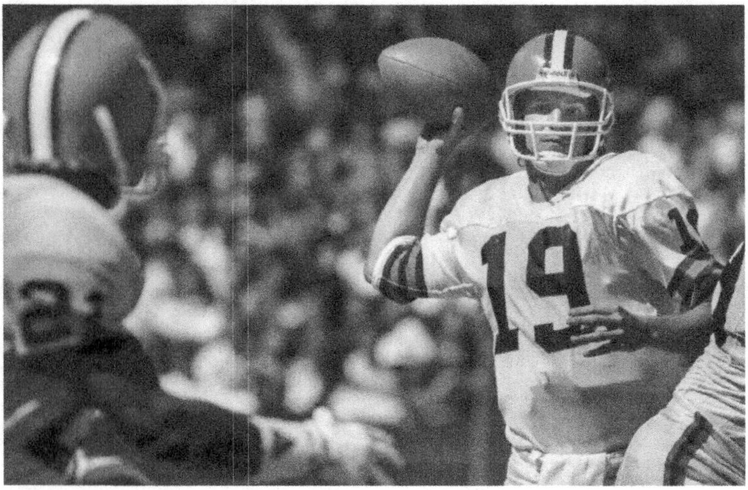

Art Modell wanted to draft Doug Flutie. General manager Ernie Accorsi pushed for Kosar and came up with a way to grab him in the supplemental draft. *David I. Andersen / The Plain Dealer*

nie's advisor (also a dentist), God bless him. He made it clear Bernie wanted to go to the Browns."

* * *

Buffalo had the first pick in the regular 1985 draft. The Bills had Jim Kelly at quarterback, so they didn't need Kosar. Buffalo already had its heart set on defensive end Bruce Smith, so the Bills weren't about to trade the No. 1 pick.

Houston had the No. 2 pick. Accorsi tried to make a deal with the Oilers, but couldn't. Houston had a star named Warren Moon at quarterback. The Oilers should have been open to a trade, but Accorsi couldn't find common ground for a deal.

During all this, Modell kept asking Accorsi about Doug Flutie.

"What does he have to do to impress you?" Modell would say.

"Art, I know Flutie's throwing for a million yards," Accorsi would reply. "But Art, I want Kosar."

Before the regular draft, Minnesota traded with Houston for the No. 2 pick. The Vikings wanted Kosar.

"As a kid, the Vikings were my second favorite team after the Browns," said Kosar. "(Minnesota coach) Bud Grant called me. I loved him as a coach. At that point, I wasn't sure what I wanted to do. I was getting in over my head."

The Browns still were obsessed with acquiring Kosar. The Kosar family still wanted the Browns.

"Bernie's first allegiance back then was always to his father," said Byrne. "He'd often say, 'You need to talk to my dad.' "

The Browns knew this. And they knew his father, Bernie Kosar Sr., would help them.

Accorsi came up with the idea of having Kosar skip the regular 1985 NFL Draft, but apply for the "supplemental draft." It happens after the NFL draft and usually it's not a big deal.

So Kosar held off graduating and delayed turning in his paperwork to the NFL until after the April 30 regular draft. Houston, Minnesota and other teams were outraged when they figured out what was happening. They complained to the NFL.

Commissioner Pete Rozelle met with the interested parties and ruled in favor of Kosar entering the supplemental draft.

The Browns completed a trade with Buffalo, which also had the first pick in the supplemental draft.

"We made the trade before we knew for sure Bernie was going into the supplemental draft," said Accorsi. "We never talked to Bernie during that time. We knew he wanted to play for the Browns, but I was sweating it. What if he went back to Miami?"

Accorsi sent Buffalo a pair of first-round picks, a third-round pick and a sixth-rounder for the anticipated rights to Kosar.

On July 2, 1985, Kosar officially joined the Browns.

TWO RECEIVERS: REGGIE LANGHORNE AND BRIAN BRENNAN

This book is not about the best players who ever played for the Browns, although many of the great ones can be found in these pages. It's about guys whose careers said something about the heart of the team.

Two of them are Brian Brennan and Reggie Langhorne.

Neither made a Pro Bowl. Neither was highly valued in the NFL draft. Neither ever wanted to leave the Browns, at least until Bill Belichick showed up and delivered them a frozen shoulder and a finger pointed in the direction of the door.

Both still live in the Cleveland area. Both are engaging guys who treasure their time in an orange helmet.

Reggie Langhorne and Brian Brennan. Here are their stories.

* * *

"I just realized I've been selling cars longer than I played in the NFL."

That's what Reggie Langhorne said when explaining how he came to the Browns.

Langhorne is in his 10th year with Serpentini Chevrolet of Westlake. He spent nine years catching passes for the Browns and Indianapolis, his last pro season being 1993.

"The NFL?" said Langhorne. "I never thought about that. No one did in my home town. I didn't even plan to go to college. I was ready to join the Army after high school."

Home is Smithfield, Va., about 10 miles from Newport News in the eastern part of the state. The population is now about 8,500. It was about 3,500 when Langhorne was growing up there in the 1970s.

Smithfield does have a claim to fame . . . It's the "Ham Capital of the World," home of Smithfield Foods Inc.

"It's hard to explain how small my town was when I was growing up," said Langhorne. "I never went to an NFL game. I never met a pro player. I was surrounded by athletes in my family. But the pros? Never even imagined it."

Langhorne's father was a welder in Newport News. His mother worked for General Electric.

"We were blue collar folks," he said. "They built a house in 1971. Still live there. My grandmother lived next door. My sister lived across the street."

* * *

Brian Brennan had plans. He attended Boston College, but not as a road to the NFL.

"I went for education," said Brennan. "I was a finance major. I was president of a student group in the Carroll School of Management. I was trying to get all those resume fillers."

He was thinking business. He was thinking about wearing a suit and tie, dealing with clients, talking money. He was being realistic. As a college senior, he was 5-foot-9 and 170 pounds. Great size for a future bank manager. He also was winner of the Boston College Eagle Award as the school's top student-athlete. On the night of the draft, he received that honor at a banquet.

What happened to those plans?

"What happened was Doug Flutie showed up and suddenly

we're winning, playing on national TV and I'm catching all these passes from him," said Brennan.

And he became an NFL prospect.

* * *

Brennan was thinking about college before he even entered the first grade—it was expected in his family. For Langhorne, it was a different story.

"I didn't like school," said Langhorne. "I didn't like going to class. But Coach Buggs thought I should go to college. He went to Elizabeth City, so I went there."

Coach Buggs was Joe Buggs, the high school coach of Langhorne.

"My mother said going to college couldn't hurt," recalled Langhorne. "She said the Army would always be there if I wanted it."

Wise mother.

"I was finally out of my little town," said Langhorne. "I had been with the same set of girls since Head Start through the 12th grade. We played schools from different places. We had crowds around 3,000."

It was fun. It was different. Even school was OK.

When Langhorne was playing for Elizabeth City (1981-85), the United States Football League (USFL) became a factor for players at smaller schools.

The USFL existed only from 1983-85, but it created 18 new pro teams. More jobs for football players.

"In 1983, we played against Norfolk State," said Langhorne. "They were one of the highest ranked Division II schools in the country. I caught something like eight passes for 171 yards and was the MVP of the game. They had some big time players and I could compete against them."

Scouts were at that game. They wrote down Langhorne's name.

Brian Brennan scores his first NFL touchdown, a 14-yard pass from Paul McDonald at the Stadium in 1984. He attended Boston College for an education, not a football career. But he just kept catching passes. *Richard T. Conway / The Plain Dealer*

Elizabeth City is one of the Historically Black Colleges and Universities. It had already sent two players to the USFL.

"Scouts had come to our school to work them out," said Langhorne. "They said they'd come see me next year."

And they did.

"There were no pro days or anything," said Langhorne. "Some scouts would call the dorm at 11 in the morning for me to work out."

Langhorne said a few scouts would show up at the same time. They were traveling together, stopping at the small schools to check out prospects.

"There were days when I went out for pizza at lunch, came back and the phone rang—a scout was in town," said Langhorne. "He'd want me to run a 40-yard dash. I was like, 'I just ate 8-9 pieces of pizza.' So I ran the 40. Didn't matter if I was tired, sore or what. You did what they asked."

* * *

On NFL draft day in 1984, Brian Brennan sat in his dorm room at Boston College.

At the studios of a 5-year-old network called ESPN, Mel Kiper Jr. was making his first televised draft appearance. He was 23 years old and being paid $400 to work the draft.

"I thought I would at least be a second-round pick," said Brennan. "Irving Fryar was the top pick in the draft. Kenny Jackson went fourth. They were the two top receivers. I thought I'd go after them."

Brennan had a sensational senior season at Boston College as the favorite receiver for Doug Flutie. He caught 66 passes in 11 games, eight for TDs, and averaged 17.4 yards per reception. He also averaged 8.1 yards per punt return.

He was a second-team All-America receiver, but he was listed at only 5-foot-9, 175 pounds. Not exactly the size the NFL wants at any position.

"There were two or three NFL combines that year," said Brennan. "I took part in all of them. I excelled in things like the box drill and other agility drills. I was pretty strong in the bench press."

Several NFL teams talked to him.

As he settled into his room to watch the NFL draft, he believed it wouldn't be long until his name was called.

"Fourth round," said Brennan. "I was the 104th player picked."

Brennan said most of his senior classmates were wandering around campus. A few would stop at his room and ask, "Get picked yet?"

"Not yet," he said.

Over and over, it was "No . . . No . . . No."

After a while, he'd just say, "Not yet" when someone stopped by. There were nine receivers picked prior to Brennan.

The draft wasn't covered like now with every pick analyzed. ESPN would break away from the draft for a while to other programming.

"You'd see names of guys drafted crawling on the bottom of the screen," Brennan said. "The draft was 12 rounds back then. I was sitting there thinking I was a better player than Kenny Jackson, and he went fourth overall."

Finally, the Browns took him in the fourth round. Brennan was the 10th receiver picked in that draft.

Only two of them—Louis Lipps and Fryar—had more career NFL receptions than Brennan. And yes, Brennan was right about being superior to Kenny Jackson, who had 126 career receptions compared to 334 for Brennan.

* * *

Langhorne didn't have ESPN or cable TV when he was waiting for his name to be called in the 1985 draft, the year after Brennan was picked by the Browns.

"I was drafted by the Oakland Invaders (USFL), but that league was coming to an end," said Langhorne. "My agent and I met with them, but decided it wasn't even worth talking about a contract."

So he waited for the NFL draft.

"On draft day, I went over to my grandmother's house and sat on the porch," he said. "There was no way for me to follow the draft. I was mostly living with my granny at that time."

Browns scout Dom Anile had been to Elizabeth City several times to see Langhorne. The scout said the Browns wanted him. But who knew if that would happen?

At noon, Langhorne called his agent. He wanted to know if the draft was over and what happened.

"They're still in the first round," the agent said.

It showed how little Langhorne knew about the draft process.

"When I was invited to the NFL Combine, I had no idea what that was," said Langhorne. "I wasn't a guy who watched a lot of college football on TV, or the pros. I just knew guys got drafted."

And at 5 p.m., Langhorne's mother showed up.

"I think it's one of those football guys calling you," she said.

Langhorne said he "ran" over to his mother's house.

"Reginald, this is Dom Anile," said the man on the phone.

"How ya' doin'?" asked Langhorne.

"The Jets are up next," said Anile. "We're in the seventh round. If the Jets don't take you, we'll be calling you right back."

"OK," said Langhorne. "That's pretty cool."

Then Langhorne went back to Grandma's porch.

"Fifteen minutes later, they called back," said Langhorne.

"Reginald," said Anile. "Welcome to Cleveland. You just got drafted in the seventh round. You'll be coming to Cleveland in 48 hours, so get your stuff ready."

Then Langhorne was put on hold for a few minutes. The next thing he knew, he was on the speaker phone talking to the Cleveland media.

"I'd never talked to more than one reporter at a time," said Langhorne. "Everything was new to me."

He was the 175th pick in that draft. His signing bonus was $29,000.

"That's all that was guaranteed," he said. "I got $15,000 more if I made the team. My first year salary was $73,000. The next year, it was $90,000."

* * *

When the phone finally rang in Brennan's room, it was Paul Warfield calling.

"We just drafted you in the fourth round," said Warfield. The former Browns great receiver was then working in the team's front office.

Brennan is from Detroit. He loved football and knew Warfield was a great receiver. A nervous Brennan said, "Paul, thank you for calling."

Warfield said he was turning the phone over to coach Sam Rutigliano.

"Oh," said Brennan. "OK. Sam . . . Sure . . . "

"Brian," said Rutigliano. "Will McDonough (former Boston Globe sportswriter) is a good friend of mine. He saw you play a lot in college. He tells me that you're my next Steve Largent, my next Fred Biletnikoff. We need a player like you. I can't wait to meet you."

Rutigliano was selling his young prospect by comparing Brennan to a pair of great receivers headed to the Hall of Fame.

But the Browns also had drafted Baylor receiver Bruce Davis in the second round. Apparently, they didn't even think Brennan was the next Bruce Davis, whose NFL career lasted one season and seven receptions.

* * *

For Langhorne, coming to Cleveland for summer training camp was a shock.

"When I got there, they had 19 receivers in mini-camp," said Langhorne. "Nineteen! Receivers all over the place. There were guys from all these big schools like Nebraska and Miami. Guys like Brian Brennan, Willis Adams . . . I didn't know where I fit."

Each day, it seemed at least one receiver was being cut. Sometimes, more.

"I knew I had to get down to the last 6-or-7 to make the team," said Langhorne. "I dropped a ball in the last preseason game. It bounced off my chest and was intercepted. I thought I would be cut."

Langhorne went to practice the next day, awaiting bad news. Instead, several media members found him in the locker room and said he'd made the team.

"A minute later, Marty (coach Marty Schottenheimer) tapped me on the shoulder," said Langhorne. "He took me outside."

Schottenheimer stared hard at Langhorne.

"Listen, I cut a veteran today to keep you," he said. "That was Dwight Walker, and Dwight's a pretty good player. I think you have the potential to be a good pro."

Schottenheimer paused.

"Listen," he said. "The minute you take this for granted . . . The minute you get comfortable and don't work hard, you're on the next train or bus back to wherever you came from in North Carolina."

As a rookie, Langhorne played mostly on special teams. When he did take the field with the offense, it often was to block. That skill helped him make the team.

By midseason, Langhorne said he began to "become too comfortable," going out a few times a week.

At midseason, a steaming Schottenheimer had a meeting with his special teams. He was unhappy with the kickoff coverage.

"I was the fastest guy on the squad," said Langhorne. "I ran a 4.32 (40-yard dash) and was supposed to be the first downfield on coverage. On the film, I was like the fourth guy down."

On film, Schottenheimer put "a red marker" on Langhorne. Schottenheimer showed how Langhorne was loafing on kickoff coverage. He then turned off the film and turned on the lights. The entire team was now in the meeting.

He made Langhorne stand up.

"Son," said Schottenheimer. "Listen to me. I want to tell you

Reggie Langhorne in 1987. He, like Brian Brennan, benefited from being covered in practice by elite cornerbacks Hanford Dixon and Frank Minnifield. *Richard T. Conway / The Plain Dealer*

something. Remember that conversation we had about eight weeks ago? Well, it's in play now."

That's all the coach said.

"After that, I was always the first guy down in coverage," said Langhorne.

* * *

It was a similar story for Brennan when he first went to training camp as a rookie.

His first contract had a $100,000 bonus, the only guaranteed money. Then he would be paid another $300,000 over three years—assuming he made the team.

"We had a minicamp at Baldwin Wallace College," said Brennan. "After the morning workout, they gave us a bag lunch. I sat down and saw Clay Matthews and Tom Cousineau. They looked like real football players."

And Brennan?

"I looked like Minnie Mouse," he said. "Part of me was wondering, what am I doing here?"

Brennan had much better hands than Minnie Mouse—or about anyone else on the team, with the exception of star tight end Ozzie Newsome.

Brennan emerged as a starting receiver near the end of the season under new head coach Marty Schottenheimer. His 35 catches were No. 2 on the team behind Newsome.

"Part of me believed I was the best athlete on the team," he said. "I'm talking wide receivers, safeties, running backs, defensive backs. Bill Cowher was the special teams coach and he had me returning punts."

When Brennan talks about his athleticism, he's giving a glimpse into his mindset. He needed that confidence and inner strength to have a significant NFL career.

The Browns' talent level quickly rose. In practice, he was being covered by Hanford Dixon and Frank Minnifield, a pair of elite Cleveland cornerbacks. That made him tougher and smarter.

The Browns' head coach had an impact on him as well.

"Marty was a student of the game," said Brennan. "He played the game. He appreciated hard work and knowing your responsibilities. I did well with Marty."

* * *

Langhorne became a starter for the Browns by 1986, his second pro season.

With Bernie Kosar at QB, the Browns had a powerhouse

offense. Along with Webster Slaughter and Brian Brennan, Langhorne gave the Browns three terrific receivers. They had a Hall of Fame tight end in Ozzie Newsome. They had running backs Kevin Mack and Earnest Byner.

Those Browns not only were good and a consistent playoff team, they were so much fun to watch.

"Bernie was so great to us," said Langhorne. "He would talk to us as a group, then individually. He knew we all wanted the ball. He had a way of making us all feel involved."

Langhorne retired after the 1993 season with the Colts. He had struggled with a drinking problem that haunted him on and off for years.

Now sober, Langhorne not only sells cars, but does some TV work for WOIO in Cleveland. He also does pre-game on field uniform inspections with former Browns defensive back Felix Wright for the NFL.

"People in Cleveland have treated me with kindness and respect," he said. "Virginia will always be my home, but after the last 10 years living here—I call Cleveland home. I love the people here."

* * *

By the middle to late 1980s, Bernie Kosar was the quarterback. Kevin Mack and Earnest Byner were in the backfield. Webster Slaughter and Reggie Langhorne joined Brennan as receivers.

"We had such a great team," said Brennan. "Being from Detroit, I understood Cleveland and the people of Cleveland. It didn't take long to feel like home. So many great memories of going to championship games. I loved it."

Brennan played eight years with the Browns (1984-91). Of the 1984 Browns draftees, only 10th-rounder Byner played more NFL games for them than Brennan.

"I was cut in the spring of 1992," said Brennan. "Bill Belichick was cleaning house."

Brennan played the next season with Cincinnati and then San Diego.

"When I was with the Chargers, they had Shawn Jefferson and Anthony Miller as receivers," said Brennan. "Those guys were like Olympic sprinters. (Linebacker) Junior Seau was such a great athlete; he could play any position."

Brennan knew he could play another year or two, but was it worth it?

"At that point, you're an older guy," he said. "They are always trying to get younger. They have a draft pick they want to play. They can cut you any time. You become expendable."

Brennan also missed Cleveland, the town and the team of the 1980s.

"Being cut by Belichick took a lot out of me," he said. "I thought I'd retire as a Brown . . . "

His voice trailed off.

"It just took a lot out of me," he repeated. "I was so proud to be a Brown and to be part of all those winning teams."

Brennan is in charge of capital marketing for KeyBank in Cleveland.

"This became home," he said. "I identified with the city, the fan base, everything. It was so special playing here."

THIS NEVER SHOULD HAVE HAPPENED: MARTY LEAVES

Imagine hearing the story of a coach who went through four different starting quarterbacks in a year. His Pro Bowl quarterback started only nine of 16 games. His star fullback missed five games. There were other significant injuries.

But that team finished with a 10-6 record and made the playoffs.

Yet, the team's owner was so frustrated with the coach that it led to the coach quitting or being fired—take your pick.

That's what happened to the Browns after the 1988 season. It happened because two stubborn men—owner Art Modell and coach Marty Schottenheimer—couldn't pause and take a deep breath. It also happened out of frustration.

In his four full seasons as the Browns head coach, Schottenheimer had records of 8-8, 12-4, 10-5 and 10-6. Playoffs all four years. Mixed into all the winning were The Fumble and The Drive, two heart-crushing, stomach-churning losses to Denver in the playoffs.

"I blame myself for this," said Ernie Accorsi, who was general manager at the time. "I should have figured out a way to save the situation."

That 1988 Browns team faced the Oilers in the first round of the playoffs, losing 24-23. Career backups Don Strock and Mike Pagel played because starting QB Bernie Kosar was injured. Strock started and left the game in the second quarter with a wrist injury. It was a mess.

Making it more frustrating, the Browns had defeated Houston 28-23 a week earlier.

"We lost by one point on Christmas Eve in the playoffs," said Accorsi. "One point! We had six different quarterback injuries that year, leading us to start four different quarterbacks. Bernie got hurt. Gary Danielson got hurt. Pagel and Don Strock got hurt twice. It was a nightmare."

The Browns were 6-3 with Kosar starting that season. Accorsi said Kosar would have been healthy enough to start the next playoff game, assuming the Browns won.

"Marty did the greatest coaching job I've ever been around," said Accorsi.

Former Browns public relations director Kevin Byrne shared the same lament as Accorsi about losing quarterbacks during that season.

"We were so desperate, Ernie found Don Strock working at a golf course," said Byrne. "He was a club pro. He came in with a pot belly. He hadn't been playing football."

Strock was 37 years old. He was with Miami in 1987, but threw only 23 passes. He had been a backup to Dan Marino. Strock had not started a game since 1983. That was five years before being imported by the Browns and immediately tossed into the lineup. The Browns won both of his starts.

"I still don't know how we won 10 games," said Byrne. "Then we lost a heartbreaker (24-23) to Houston in the playoffs. After the game, Art Modell said he wanted to meet with Marty the next day."

Byrne said earlier in the week, Schottenheimer had promised

Marty Schottenheimer leaves field after losing to Denver in the 1987 AFC Championship game. *David I. Andersen / The Plain Dealer*

to take his wife and kids to a resort. That was assuming the Browns lost. They'd begin a vacation on Christmas Day.

"Everyone was exhausted by what we went through that season," said Byrne. "That was especially true for Marty. But not Art. He was fresh. He wanted to start talking about next year, right away."

According to Accorsi, Schottenheimer told Modell of his vacation plans. They could have the big meetings when he returned in a few weeks.

"I'll refund all your money for you for the vacation," said Modell. "I don't want you to go on vacation. I want you here."

Byrne tried to intervene before the coach/owner meeting.

"I knew what was coming," said Byrne. "We had lost (offensive coordinator) Lindy Infante before the season to Green Bay, where he became head coach. Rather than hire another offensive coordinator, Marty called the plays and (assistant) Joe Pendry helped him."

But there was more.

Kurt (brother of Marty) Schottenheimer was the special teams coach.

"Art wanted Kurt reassigned or something," said Accorsi.

This was going to be bad. Real bad. Accorsi knew it. Byrne knew it.

Making it worse, Modell gave an interview to The Plain Dealer not long after the game about the need to make coaching staff changes. The owner also called Kosar "the most important part of the team."

Schottenheimer wasn't an egotist. But he knew the coach had to be viewed as the most important voice on the team. The quarterback was crucial, but it was the coach who set the tone, made the rules.

Now, they call it "culture." Well, Schottenheimer had created a culture of winning.

This was the Browns' best playoff run since the 1950s and 1960s under Paul Brown and Blanton Collier. Schottenheimer read the story and correctly perceived Modell had little appreciation for what was required from the coaches simply to make the playoffs.

* * *

Hanging over the franchise after the 1988 playoff loss was frustration. Especially for Modell, who was obsessed with taking his team to the Super Bowl. Yes, Modell won a title in 1964. He made a gutsy move by firing Paul Brown and replacing him with Blanton Collier before the 1963 season. But that title was viewed as a remnant of the Paul Brown regime. Collier was Brown's top assistant. Most of the players had been acquired by Brown.

More recently, Modell had made the right move by replacing Sam Rutigliano with Schottenheimer in the middle of the 1984 season. The Browns had pulled off an amazing supplemental draft deal bringing Kosar to Cleveland in 1985. The Schottenheimer/Kosar combination won big.

But in Modell's mind, they didn't win the Big One. They lost twice to Denver in AFC title games after the 1986 and 1987 seasons.

"I don't know if people were spoiled or what," said Accorsi. "But that 10-6 record was looked at as a disappointment when it was a remarkable achievement."

Had the Browns lost that Oilers playoff game with Kosar at quarterback, then some of this would make sense. But Mike Pagel played most of the game. This was the same Mike Pagel who had a 15-31-1 record with the Colts from 1982-85.

But all of that was lost in the gloomy storm clouds hanging over the franchise after the previous two playoff losses. Modell had been reading stories second-guessing Schottenheimer for quite a while.

Some of Modell's friends were critical of the coach.

A theme emerged: Schottenheimer was a good coach, but not a great one. He wasn't the guy who could lead the team to the Super Bowl because he was too stubborn to make needed changes.

* * *

Byrne planned the end of season press conference for the day after Christmas. Schottenheimer would speak to the media, followed by some of the players. Then everyone would go on vacation. He explained this to Modell.

"OK," said the owner. "But I want to talk to Marty."

Byrne also knew what was coming, that Modell planned to push for coaching staff changes. He called Schottenheimer with a plan.

"Art wants to talk to you," said Byrne. "Here's my suggestion. Tell him you're going to do the press conference, then leave town with your family. He'll be disappointed, but you call tell him you need some time to collect yourself after the season. You know you should do this. You know what the conversation is going to be about. You're tired. He's anxious. It's not going to work out well."

"I can handle it," said Schottenheimer. "I'll handle it."

Schottenheimer was steaming about Modell telling The Plain Dealer about making coaching changes without talking to him first.

"I should have found a way to postpone that meeting until after Marty's vacation," said Accorsi. "I should have pushed hard for that."

But Accorsi didn't.

* * *

Modell, Schottenheimer and Accorsi met at 10 a.m. The press conference was set up for 11 a.m.

"It really came down to Marty's brother," said Accorsi.

Modell wanted Schottenheimer to demote his brother. Schottenheimer was emotionally drained by the season and angry at his boss.

Byrne was summoned into the meeting. Stone cold silence greeted him as Schottenheimer and Modell glared at each other.

"Marty's going to leave," Modell said.

"WHAT?" bellowed Byrne.

"I'm not resigning," said Schottenheimer.

"I'm not firing him," said Modell.

"Wait a minute," said Byrne. "What does this mean?"

"We just have a difference here on where we want to go," said Modell. "There's no hard feelings. We're just not on the same page."

"What are we going to tell people?" asked Byrne. "How do we tell people THAT?"

"It's like Art said," said Schottenheimer. "We just disagree on some football things. It's not going to work. He believes one thing, I believe another. Maybe it's best we just part."

"Let me think about this for a moment," said Byrne.

Schottenheimer spoke to the media on Dec. 26. There was no mention of a possible coaching change. The next day—Dec. 27—the Browns announced the end of Schottenheimer's tenure as coach.

"I was frankly satisfied I did a good enough job (as offensive coordinator)," said Schottenheimer.

"That might be his perception," Modell said a day later. "I might have a different one."

Modell then added this: "I see the Oilers and Bengals franchises surging ahead and I see us almost treading water. If I were to handicap next year, we would be the third favorite in our division. That's not good enough."

Cincinnati, a franchise started by Paul Brown, won the AFC Central with a 12-4 record in 1988. Houston and the Browns were 10-6.

Modell also wanted to change some of the scouting methods used for the college draft. He blamed Schottenheimer for the dismal first-round selection of Mike "Mad Dog In A Meat Market" Junkin in 1987.

At this point, both men were spouting off reasons of why they no longer wanted to work with each other.

* * *

After the press conference, Byrne had separate conversations with Schottenheimer and Modell.

"Art said I could keep my brother and keep Joe Pendry," Schottenheimer told Byrne. "He then said he'd give me more money to hire a different special teams coach and an offensive coordinator. I don't think that's in our best interest."

Here was Modell's version to Byrne.

"Marty is so stubborn," said Modell. "I told him he can keep his brother. He can keep Pendry. Just add people to his staff. Get a special teams guru. They're out there. Add an offensive coordinator."

There was no misunderstanding on what both parties wanted. Schottenheimer insisted on no changes. Modell demanded changes.

"If Marty had gone on vacation and rested up, we could have worked this out when he got back," said Accorsi. "But not then. Not right after the game."

To be fair to Modell, the Browns had problems on special teams in 1988. There were better special teams coaches available than Kurt Schottenheimer.

Perhaps Schottenheimer would have been open to a compromise: His brother keeps his job, but the Browns hire an offensive coordinator.

But when people are exhausted and angry, no one compromises. When a steely-willed coach such as Schottenheimer felt backed into a corner to defend a family member, he was not about to back down.

Furthermore, despite all the injuries on offense, the coaching staff had found a way to win 10 games even with the team ranking 20th in scoring and 18th in total yards.

"The quarterback position is the most important in football," said Byrne. "And we got to the playoffs using four different quarterbacks. We were such a tough, disciplined team. Marty couldn't understand why Art failed to see that."

The players were stunned and crushed by what happened.

Marty Schottenheimer after a game in Jan. 1988. Owner Art Modell soured on his coach after the team lost twice to Denver in the AFC championship game. *C.H. Pete Copeland / The Plain Dealer*

They were thinking with Kosar healthy in 1989 and adding some new players, they were the same Super Bowl contenders as they had been the previous three years.

"Ernie thought they needed to make some changes on the coaching staff," said Byrne. "He had convinced Art of that."

Byrne and Accorsi both believe now that if they could have curbed Modell's compulsive need to confront the coach immediately and make changes so quickly, the Browns could have kept Schottenheimer.

"The conversations would have gone better," said Byrne. "But there was so much emotion of our hearts being ripped out in the playoffs going all the way back to Red Right 88 and all that . . . "

Byrne paused.

"We lost a great coach," he said. "And we ended up with a coach (Bud Carson) who was a very good guy, but not a good head coach."

Three weeks after leaving the Browns, Schottenheimer was

hired by Kansas City. He took over a 4-11-1 team and went 8-7-1 in his first season. To prove a point, he took Joe Pendry (now officially offensive coordinator) and Kurt Schottenheimer (special teams coach) to the Chiefs. They also had Bill Cowher as defensive coordinator and Tony Dungy as defensive backs coach. Both are now Hall of Fame coaches. Another future big name on that staff was Bruce Arians as running backs coach.

In 10 years with the Chiefs, Schottenheimer had only one losing season. He went to the playoffs seven times.

The Browns turned to Carson as head coach. He was 57 years old. He had never been a head coach in the NFL before. He had been Pittsburgh's defensive coordinator in the 1970s. His last stop was with the Jets in that same job. Carson was 9-6-1 in his first season as head coach of the Browns. But in 1990 the Browns started 2-7 and Carson was fired just past the midpoint of the 1990 season.

That set up the hiring of Bill Belichick.

BILL BELICHICK COMES TO CLEVELAND

After the breakup between head coach Marty Schottenheimer and owner Art Modell following the 1988 season, Kevin Byrne sensed the Browns were in trouble.

"We knew we'd lost a great coach," said the Browns former public relations director. "Then we hired Bud Carson . . . "

Byrne's voice trailed off as he thought about what happened after that.

But let's back up a bit to just before Carson was hired. A little-known story about the Cleveland coaching search following Schottenheimer's departure is how a 36-year-old Bill Belichick tried to get the job in 1989.

Belichick had been an assistant in Detroit and Denver before joining the New York Giants and head coach Ray Perkins. He later coached under Bill Parcells. By 1988, Belichick had risen to defensive coordinator with head coaching aspirations.

Once the Cleveland job opened up, he called Browns general manager Ernie Accorsi, asking for an interview. The two had met before.

"Bill came to Baltimore as an intern when I was working there (in 1975)," said Accorsi. "(Colts Coach) Ted Marchibroda raved about Bill, who was only there a year."

"I told Bill that I'd pretty much made up my mind, but we could have lunch at the Senior Bowl," recalled Accorsi, who had his eye on veteran defensive coordinator Bud Carson.

Accorsi planned to spend an hour at lunch with Belichick.

They talked through lunch, dinner and into the early evening.

"The interview was spectacular," said Accorsi. "I was blown away by him. It was like he had been preparing to be a head coach since he was 6 years old. That probably was the case, because he was watching film with his dad (coach Steve Belichick) when he was a little kid."

It's hard to imagine Belichick being dynamic in interviews, but I have heard that story about him from other people at different stages of his career.

When Belichick wanted to be personable and expansive, he could do it—and come across as confident and prepared.

"He was a defensive coach who had thought a lot about offense," said Accorsi. "He had a distinct philosophy. He believed you win games over the middle."

Meaning what?

"He wanted guys who could catch the ball in the middle of the field," said Accorsi. "He said defenses were designed to protect the outside, but the middle of the field was open."

Belichick wanted big linemen to open the middle of the field with their blocks on offense, and big defensive linemen to shut it down when on defense.

"After that interview, I told Bill it was like he was in a golf tournament where he started the day 15 strokes back and ended up right behind the leader," said Accorsi. "He gave me a lot to think about. But in the end, I went with Bud."

* * *

Bud was 57-year-old Leon "Bud" Carson who had been in the NFL for 17 years, but never as a head coach. When talking to

Accorsi, keep in mind Baltimore is his frame of reference. After making the big trade for Bernie Kosar, he told the quarterback to "forget about being the next Brian Sipe, be the next Johnny Unitas."

And Carson?

"I saw him like Earl Weaver," said Accorsi. "Kind of a cantankerous genius."

Weaver was the great manager of the Baltimore Orioles, one of the earliest disciples of what grew into baseball analytics. Weaver managed at every level in the minors—for 11 years—before taking over the Orioles in the middle of the 1968 season.

Carson had been a head coach at Georgia Tech for five seasons. He moved to the NFL and made his reputation as the coordinator for Chuck Noll's "Steel Curtain" defense for five years and two Super Bowl titles in Pittsburgh. He also reached the Super Bowl as a defensive coordinator with the L.A. Rams.

"I really thought about hiring Bill at that point," said Accorsi. "But we had a veteran team. We had maybe one last gasp. I had been with Bud in Baltimore (in 1982) and I thought he was absolutely brilliant as a defensive coordinator. His defenses had success against John Elway. I thought maybe we could steal it (a championship) before our team ran out of gas."

So he hired Carson.

Bud Carson was no Earl Weaver . . . nor Marty Schottenheimer . . . nor even an average coach when he came to the Browns.

"He was like an eccentric scientist," said Byrne. "He was a nice guy, but loved to watch film, work on Xs and Os. That was what he preferred to do."

Carson had a 9-6-1 record in his first season (1989) as the Browns head coach. For the third time in four years, Denver knocked the Browns out of the playoffs.

The next season, the Browns started with a 2-7 record. The team lacked discipline. The coach was often overwhelmed. There were times when he was walking off the field right after the game with Byrne and he'd ask, "What should I say to these guys?"

That's right, the head coach was seeking advice from the public relations director on what to tell the team in the locker room. A few times, Byrne made suggestions such as, "There are five games left in the season, we're a game out of the playoffs. We have plenty of time."

Then Byrne would stand in the back of the locker room as Carson stood in front of the team and said some things Byrne had told him. Byrne and others soon realized Carson didn't have the confidence in himself to be the head coach.

To follow Accorsi's baseball comparison, there are times when great pitching coaches become managers—and fail miserably. That's because their focus was on pitching.

Carson's final Browns game was a 42-0 loss to Buffalo.

* * *

The Browns finished the 1990 season with a 3-13 record.

This time, Belichick didn't need to call Accorsi. The Browns general manager sought out Belichick, who was the defensive coordinator of the 1990 Super Bowl winning New York Giants.

"At this point, Bill was hot," said Accorsi. "Everyone was raving about him as being the next great head coach. I wanted him and went after him."

Belichick was still interested in Cleveland. He already had Accorsi's endorsement. The next step was to spend the evening with Art and Pat Modell at their home. Indiana basketball coach Bob Knight had called Modell, raving about Belichick. They had become friends over the years, and Knight's endorsement excited Modell.

Then came "the binder." That's what those with the Browns would later name it.

It was a large notebook in which Belichick had written out pre-

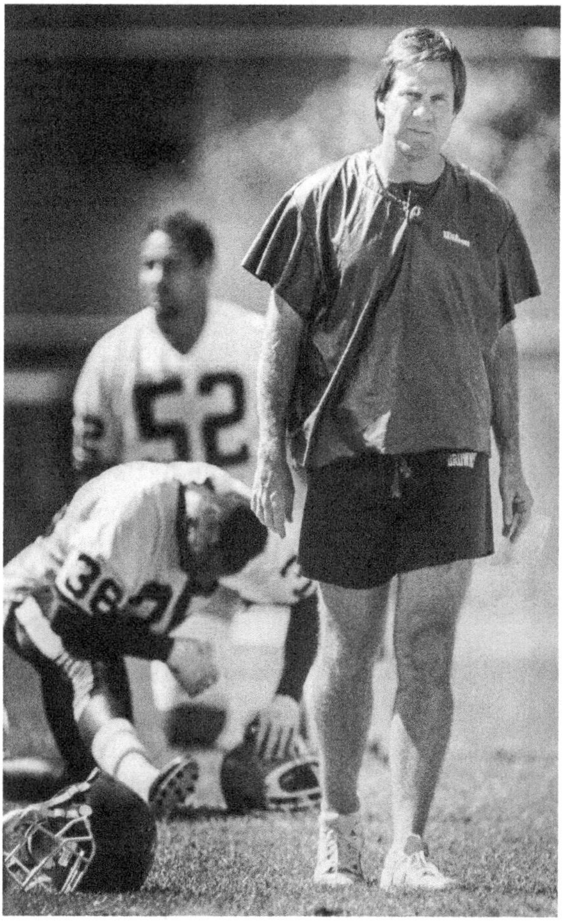

Bill Belichick wanted complete control of the football organization, and Modell gave it to him. Here, he leads a Browns minicamp in 1991. *Chris Stephens / The Plain Dealer*

cisely what it would take to turn around the Browns. He stressed the need to have three Pro Bowlers on offense, three on defense—at minimum. He was blunt about how the Browns were being perceived across the NFL as a soft, aging, undisciplined team. Belichick's plan was for the Browns to get bigger. Bigger linemen. Bigger receivers. Bigger backs.

Soon, Modell was telling everyone how Belichick "has it figured out. I've never talked to a coach who has it planned out like Bill."

In 1994, I did a long interview with Belichick. He made this point, one he stressed with the Modells in his interview at their home.

"When I came here, we had few players in the 5-to-8 year range—the prime of their careers," he said. "We had guys in the 10-year range, or younger players."

His plan was to rip up the roster. It was going to be painful the first few years, but it would pay off.

"We had to rebuild the entire organization," Belichick told me. "Not just the players, but the coaches and scouts."

And he didn't stop there. He also changed the locker room, the practice fields and offices.

* * *

Modell had a dream ever since he fired Paul Brown after the 1962 season.

The owner wanted to find his own Paul Brown.

To this day, Belichick considers Paul Brown the greatest football coach ever because of his innovations. Brown and Belichick's father, Steve Belichick, were good friends.

Paul Brown had complete power to run the Browns while winning seven titles (before he clashed with Modell after the brash New Yorker bought the Browns).

Belichick wanted that kind of complete control of the football organization, and Modell gave it to him. At the press conference announcing the hiring of Belichick, Modell said the new coach would have "total consultation and input into the draft." He'd also talk directly to the owner.

Accorsi (who was already thinking about leaving the team because his mother was ill) was being moved aside.

Belichick was given a 5-year contract.

Belichick began to bring in young coaches: Nick Saban, Steve Crosby and Scott O'Brien. More would come. The early practices were brutal, twice a day in pads. Browns veterans were shocked.

In the first few years, he began dumping fan favorites such as Brian Brennan, Kevin Mack, Webster Slaughter and Reggie Langhorne.

Belichick was rude with the media and had no interest in improving that relationship, despite Byrne making suggestions and trying to help. He was equally dismissive of many of the players.

Belichick's attitude was based on having won two Super Bowls in New York. In comparison, the Browns had won nothing. He had little respect for what the Browns players of the late 1980s had accomplished, or what they meant to the Cleveland fans. In his view, they couldn't help him win now—and how can others fail to be smart enough to see that?

In press conferences, he could be rude and dismissive of questions. That works if you are an established head coach and winning, not a "rookie head coach," as Belichick was in 1991. He hated that term, so several in the media used it next to his name to annoy him.

To the Browns players and many fans, he was just that—a rookie head coach. Who was Belichick to have such an elitist attitude? Bill Parcells was the head coach in New York when the Giants won those Super Bowls, not Belichick. Nor had Belichick ever played in the NFL.

When hired at the age of 38, he was the youngest head coach in the NFL and not much older than some of his players.

"I was cut in the spring of 1992," said Brian Brennan. "Bill was cleaning house."

Brennan didn't see it coming. He was 30 years old and had

caught 31 passes the season before. Brennan said he was summoned to Coach Belichick's office. Belichick was behind his desk. He barely made eye contact. After an awkward silence, the coach spoke.

"Brian, I'm looking for a more physical receiver," Belichick said. "You are a finesse player. You've been a good player, but we're moving forward."

Brennan's voice still reflected the pain as he told the story 30 years later.

"I was standing there," said Brennan. "He stared at me. I looked at him. No one said anything. Then I left."

* * *

In Belichick's first season as head coach of the Browns, star receiver Reggie Langhorne was holding out for a new contract. In 1990, Langhorne and Brennan each had 45 receptions.

"As I started to miss training camp, Bill began taking money off the table from what he offered me," said Langhorne. "Eventually, I signed and came to camp. He wasn't happy with me. He wanted me to be at 200 pounds and I weighed 202. He fined me $50 a pound."

Belichick also dropped Langhorne on the depth chart, making him work with the scout team. Langhorne believed Belichick was unfairly punishing him over their contract dispute.

Langhorne refused to work out with the scout team. He walked off the field and sat on top of his helmet, watching practice from the sideline.

Ozzie Newsome and receivers coach Richard Mann came up to Langhorne and asked him to join the scout team.

"Forget it," said Langhorne. "Then they went to get Web (fellow receiver Webster Slaughter) to talk to me, but Web told them, 'I'm with Reggie.' So I didn't go back into practice. But I also didn't leave the facility."

An enraged Belichick fined Langhorne $15,000 "for not hustling in practice."

A furious Langhorne went to see Accorsi after practice. He begged the general manager to trade him. Then he ran into a reporter, who had heard about what happened on the field. He asked Langhorne if the receiver wanted to be traded. Langhorne said he did. That became a big story the next day.

Belichick saw the paper, exploded and fined Langhorne another $30,000. The coach said the receiver would not go to New York for that weekend's game with the Giants.

"Suddenly, I was fined $45,000," said Langhorne.

Langhorne's agent and the Players Association filed a grievance, and won. A key piece of evidence was that Langhorne's teammate Michael Dean Perry had walked out of practice and left the building. The defensive lineman was fined only $200.

Langhorne received a check for $44,800. They held back $200, the same amount Perry paid.

"He was a young coach," said Langhorne. "We have since made up. I now speak well of Bill to everyone. I don't hold to any of those old resentments."

Belichick took over a 3-13 team and was 6-10 and 7-9 in his first two seasons as Cleveland's head coach.

Then came 1993, and the move that shocked the fans and the city.

BILL & BERNIE

Today, Bill Belichick and Bernie Kosar have a good relationship. It has been that way for years.

"Bill and I made up not long after he got the New England job," said Kosar. "I was interviewed by some writers when he was hired, and I told them I thought Bill would be a good coach. I meant it. He's a smart guy."

There's more.

"Bill called to thank me," said Kosar. "We've been friends ever since. I try not to carry grudges for long."

There's even more.

When the Browns were looking for coaching candidates before their return in 1999, Kosar suggested Belichick for the job in a meeting with Browns owner Al Lerner and team president Carmen Policy. Belichick was the defensive coordinator with the Jets at the time.

This was six years after Belichick cut Kosar.

Policy exploded that it would be a public relations nightmare to bring Belichick back to Cleveland.

* * *

All of this might be hard to believe when you look back at what happened between Kosar and Belichick in 1993.

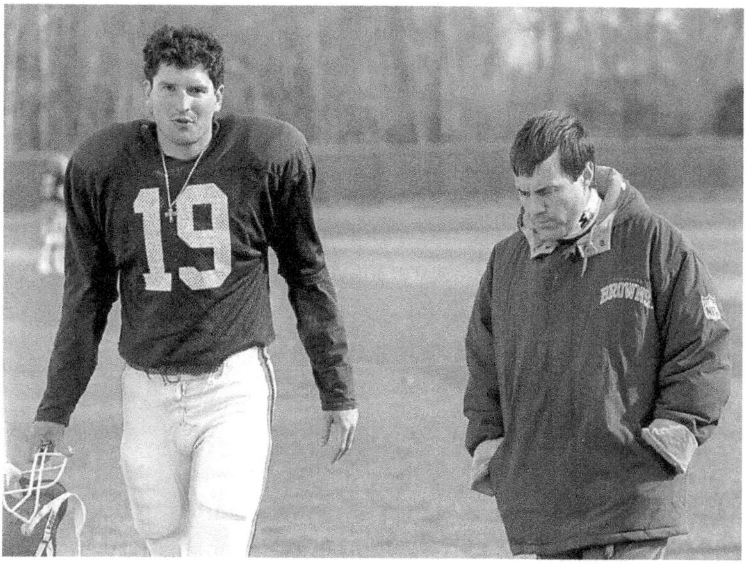

Bernie Kosar walks with Bill Belichick during practice in October 1993. It would be Kosar's last season with the Browns. *David I. Andersen / The Plain Dealer*

People who know this era of Browns history remember Belichick's infamous assessment of Kosar: "Diminishing skills."

But if we look back objectively, Belichick was right about Kosar. The quarterback's skills were diminishing.

Belichick was hired before the 1991 season. He inherited Kosar at starting quarterback, and the two men had a decent start to their relationship.

Kosar played all 16 games in 1991, and the Browns were 6-10. That was an improvement over 3-13 in the previous season. Kosar threw for 3,487 yards, the third highest total of his career. He also delivered 18 TD passes compared to eight interceptions.

Kosar was the starting quarterback in 1992, but broke his ankle late in the first half of a 27-23 loss to Miami. Kosar knew his ankle was injured, but didn't find out about the fracture until after the game. He played the entire second half on a broken ankle.

The Browns finished the season 7-9. Mike Tomczak took over at starting quarterback for Kosar and had a 4-4 record. That led to Belichick thinking about a quarterback change for 1993.

This is where it becomes ugly.

After the 1992 season, the Browns came to Kosar and asked him to rework his contract. The idea was to give the team some salary cap relief and add some players.

Kosar agreed.

The Browns did indeed add a significant free agent.

His name was Vinny Testaverde.

The same Vinny Testaverde who had been the backup quarterback to Kosar at the University of Miami in 1984. After Kosar graduated, Testaverde became the Hurricanes' starter and eventually the No. 1 pick in the 1987 NFL draft. He spent six seasons with Tampa Bay. His record as a starter was 24-48 with 77 TD passes compared to 112 interceptions.

Kosar couldn't believe that some of the changes made to his contract were leading to his replacement at quarterback. Testaverde signed a $1.7 million deal that could be worth $2.5 million with various incentives.

The Browns tried to spin it that Testaverde would be the backup. After all, Kosar had been injured several times over the years.

But Kosar knew Bill Belichick liked big, strong, physical players at almost every position. That included the quarterback. At 6-foot-5 and 235 pounds, Testaverde was a big, strong, physical quarterback who also was very mobile.

At this point, Belichick should have just waived Kosar before the season opened to avoid a nasty quarterback controversy. But Belichick brought Kosar and Testaverde to training camp. I remember watching training camp and a few preseason games in 1993. Testaverde was a physical marvel in terms of arm strength and mobility, far superior to Kosar. Meanwhile, Kosar was coming off a broken ankle. Also, we now know he had suffered multiple concussions, too—something ignored back then.

Why did Belichick open the 1993 season with Kosar when he seemed to believe Testaverde was better?

"Bernie had been the starter and I didn't think it would be fair to take the job away from him based on four preseason games," Belichick told me a few months after the 1993 season ended.

* * *

The 1993 season opened with Kosar starting and Belichick believing Testaverde was the better choice. The Browns won their first two games by scores of 27-14 and 23-13. Kosar was solid. In the third game Kosar struggled, throwing three interceptions. The Browns were down 13-0 early in the fourth quarter when Testaverde replaced Kosar. Cleveland came back to beat the Raiders, 19-16.

Kosar started the fourth game of the season, but was replaced by Testaverde. The Browns lost 23-10 to the Colts. In the fifth game, Kosar started. Testaverde relieved. The Browns lost again. Testaverde started the next two games—victories over Cincinnati and Pittsburgh.

But late in the Pittsburgh game, Testaverde suffered a separated shoulder.

That led to Kosar starting against Denver in Game 8 of the season. The Browns lost 29-14. But late in that game, Kosar ignored a play call from the coaches. He "drew up a play in the dirt," Kosar said. That led to a 38-yard TD pass to receiver Michael Jackson with nine seconds left in the game.

Later, I talked to someone who was on the sidelines during this game.

Belichick was frustrated about Testaverde being hurt. He was angry because Denver was winning. He was furious with Kosar.

The coach thought Kosar was dividing the team. When Kosar shook off that last play, Belichick screamed f-bombs at the quarterback. Most of the team could hear it. Kosar ignored him, throwing the touchdown pass.

After the game, Belichick was a volcano about Kosar's attitude. Kosar was dumbfounded. The play he'd concocted did lead to a touchdown. Several other big plays during the season were the result of him changing plays.

* * *

Some history is needed to understand why Kosar was so offended by Belichick refusing to allow him to change plays at the line of scrimmage.

"It goes back to college," said Kosar.

He explained that Miami coach Howard Schnellenberger "mandated" that a quarterback know his offense and the opposing defenses so well that he change the play when the play called by the coaches looked destined to fail.

"Coach Schnellenberger taught us the quarterback was there to erase mistakes," said Kosar. "That included coaches' mistakes."

His next Miami coach—Jimmy Johnson—had the same approach.

"Somehow, some way, we've got to win this game," Johnson told his quarterbacks.

To Kosar, that meant "find a way." If the way was to change the play call, or even "draw up a play in the dirt" in the huddle, do it.

In Kosar's first NFL start, in 1985, the Browns were playing in Houston.

"Houston saw me as a tall, slow guy," said Kosar. "They thought they could blitz me and pummel me in the pocket."

That's what happened in the first half. Kosar was taking a physical beating. The play calls didn't help.

Teammates and rivals. In 1993, Bernie Kosar (left) was coming off a broken ankle. Newly acquired free agent Vinny Testaverde was Bill Belichick's idea of a quarterback: big, strong, and mobile. *Scott Shaw / The Plain Dealer*

"On third down, we had Ozzie Newsome off the field," said Kosar. "We had four receivers, one running back. I was getting steamrolled by the blitzes."

At halftime, he called the offense together.

Kosar told the offense he wanted Newsome and two backs on the field in third-down passing situations. He could throw quick passes to them to negate the blitz.

Remember, this was a rookie quarterback in his first NFL start making these adjustments. The coaching staff went with it. The Browns won, 21-6. The big play was a 68-yard TD pass to Clarence Weathers, a play Kosar changed in the huddle.

From that point, Kosar not only had a major say in game-plan preparation, he also had freedom to change plays at the line of scrimmage. Kosar always was incredibly smart when it comes to football. His mind and ability to quickly adapt to the defense were part of what made him a tremendous quarterback for the Browns in the late 1980s and even with Belichick in 1991.

* * *

But this was 1993. Kosar had taken such a physical pounding over the years, he wasn't the same Bernie Kosar anymore.

Belichick would put tapes of Testaverde and Kosar next to each other, flipping back and forth as the coaching staff watched. He would grumble and then build up to a fiery tirade about how Kosar didn't have the same arm strength as Testaverde. And Testaverde was the better quarterback. And Kosar couldn't accept it. And it was Kosar dividing the team.

It went on and on and on.

After the loss to Denver, Belichick had a meeting with general manager Mike Lombardi. The coach wanted Kosar out. Now.

They went to see Art Modell. At first, the owner thought Belichick wanted to bench Kosar for the next game. With Testaverde still hurt, that meant seldom-used Todd Philcox would start.

No, the coach wanted to cut Kosar.

NOW!

Modell didn't want to do it. But he also had given Belichick a 2-year contract extension earlier in the 1993 season. The coach was under contract through 1997. Modell often said Belichick would "be my last coach."

Now Belichick—his version of Paul Brown—wanted the owner to agree to cut the team's most popular player.

"I want him out of here," said Belichick. "He is actively trying to undermine the coaching staff."

It took several hours for a final decision. But along with Jim Brown and Lombardi, Belichick sold Modell on the idea of dumping Kosar.

* * *

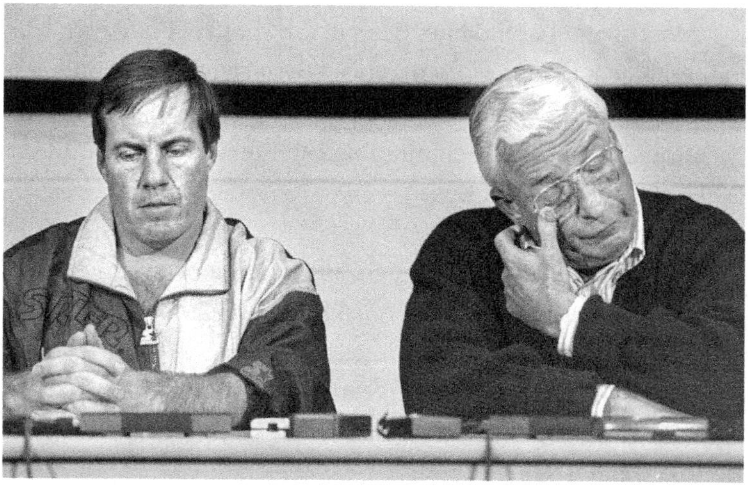

Nov. 8, 1993: Neither Bill Belichick nor Art Modell looks comfortable announcing the release of fan favorite Bernie Kosar. "A pure football decision," the Browns called it. *Gus Chan / The Plain Dealer*

The next morning, there was a meeting that included Modell, Belichick and public relations director Kevin Byrne.

Byrne wanted to know how to portray this change to the media.

Belichick wanted to know why they even needed a press conference. Just write a short press release saying Kosar was waived and give it to the media.

Modell and Byrne said they had to face the media.

That led to a discussion of what to say when explaining the decision. They didn't want to get into Belichick's claim of Kosar dividing the team.

The coach talked about Kosar's lack of arm strength and mobility, which had become a familiar mantra in Berea by now.

"So his skills have diminished," said Byrne.

Belichick agreed.

They called a press conference. To Modell's credit, he sat next to his coach.

"Most owners would have been in the South of France that day rather than at that press conference," Byrne later told people.

The Browns told the media this was "a pure football decision."

At one point, Belichick mumbled the now infamous "diminished skills" line about Kosar.

The coach was right.

"Bernie has been hurt so much, I don't know of any other quarterback who has taken more punishment," said Modell.

And the owner was right.

But cutting Kosar when the team was 5-3 and Testaverde was still out with a separated shoulder?

That was absolutely wrong.

As I wrote after the press conference: "Does anyone believe the Browns that 100 percent of Todd Philcox is better than 70 percent of Bernie Kosar?"

Philcox had been cut at the end of training camp, then re-signed as the No. 3 quarterback. When 1993 opened, Philcox was entering his fourth pro season. He had started exactly one game. He was the ideal third-string quarterback, a good guy running the scout team and helping the other two quarterbacks prepare for the game.

He was not a guy who should have been tossed into the role of replacing Kosar in the middle of the season.

I was among the reporters able to talk to Philcox that day. He was shocked by what had happened to Kosar. He seemed stunned about being suddenly put in position to start in Seattle.

I also was hearing from Browns officials how the coaches supposedly were asked to take a vote by Belichick. Did they believe the Browns had a better chance to win the next game in Seattle with Kosar or Philcox? Supposedly, all the coaches voted for Philcox.

The only way that could have been true was if the coaches

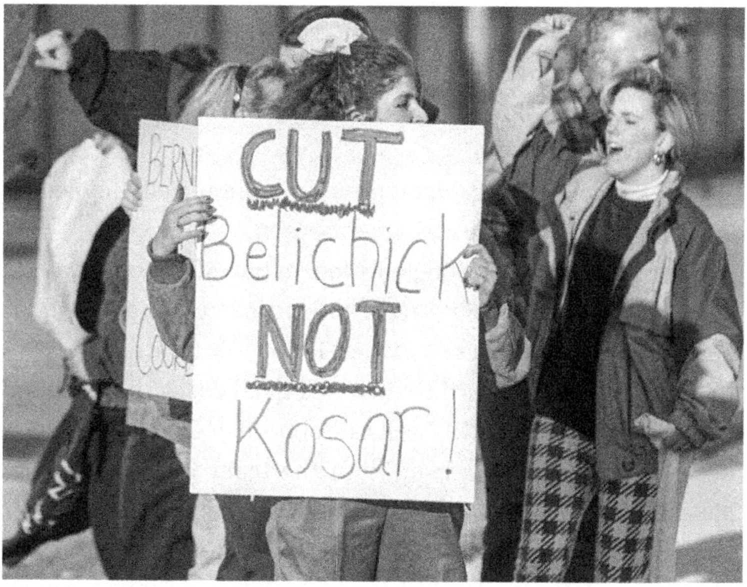

A small group of fans gathered to protest in support of Bernie Kosar outside of Browns headquarters in Berea on Nov. 8, 1993. *Gus Chan / The Plain Dealer*

voted that way because they knew Belichick was going to make the move anyway.

Meanwhile, Kosar was immediately signed by the Dallas Cowboys, who had a desperate need for a quarterback.

As the Browns were losing 22-5 in Seattle with poor Philcox completely overwhelmed, Kosar took over for starter Jason Garrett and led the Cowboys to a 20-15 win over Phoenix.

I was covering the game in Seattle. At the same time the Browns were being embarrassed on the field, a press box television set had Kosar being a hero for the Cowboys.

This was the lowest point of a very low week for Belichick and the Browns. It was why the fans developed an absolute loathing for the coach, who tried to sell them on Philcox over Kosar.

* * *

The Browns finished with a 7-9 record, 2-6 after cutting Kosar. They fell apart in the second half of the season. The mood of the fans was the most ugly I'd ever experienced in all my decades covering Cleveland sports.

It was exceeded only when the team announced the move to Baltimore in the middle of the 1995 season.

Philcox ended up starting only four games after Kosar was cut. The Browns were 1-3 while Testaverde recovered from his shoulder injury. They also were 1-3 when Testaverde returned.

It was Belichick's third season as a head coach, but he came across as inexperienced as well as stubborn. He wanted to blame Kosar for "dividing the team," but the team was 5-3 when he played.

The real division in the team came when Kosar was cut and the players knew the coach's decision had made it harder for them to win.

After the 1993 season, I had that long, in-depth interview with Belichick.

"When Vinny played, he played well," Belichick told me. "It was hard for me to look Vinny in the eye and say, 'You can't play,' so I played him."

I didn't debate the skills of Testaverde vs. Kosar in that discussion. But the timing of Kosar's departure was wrong. And the coach refused to admit it.

"The team was getting divided based on how the quarterbacks were performing," Belichick said. "As a coach, there's not much you can do about how people feel. Vinny was playing well. We were gaining confidence with Vinny."

Belichick refused to directly address the timing issue.

"It was time to move on (from Kosar)," said Belichick. "It was time to move in a new direction. We wanted to throw more downfield."

I told Belchick he was asking to be criticized.

"You have to have a sense of purpose and self confidence," he said. "You will always face adversity. If people expect me to just walk off the field, turn in my gear and quit—they don't know me. I could have done that years ago when I was a player and coaches yelled at me."

* * *

I'm ending this chapter where it started, with the reconciliation of Kosar and Belichick. I dealt with this in a 2010 Plain Dealer story.

"I got whacked by Bill, but stuff does happen," Kosar said. "You can't change history. You can't be negative or bitter about it. I didn't want to carry that around when it came to Bill. When reporters asked me about how Bill would do in New England, they figured I'd slam him. But I said what I really believed. Bill is fantastic when it comes to organization and discipline. His strength is defense. He really knows his X's and O's. He could learn offense, and he'd learn from what happened in Cleveland."

This says two things about Kosar: 1) He is a very creative thinker and risk taker when it comes to football. 2) He really hates grudges.

In his book, "Learning to Scramble," written with Craig Stout, Kosar deals little with Belichick and is very kind when he does write about him.

"In fairness to Coach Belichick, he was new and perhaps a little touchy about his command and control," wrote Kosar. "I can assure you that's no longer the case. A significant part of his success with the New England Patriots . . . has come from his complete confidence in his quarterback to do the right thing, even on the fly. Of course, such confidence may come easier if your quarterback is young Tom Brady, not old Bernie Kosar."

What about Belichick's thoughts on Kosar?

In 2010, I reached out to the coach and he responded with this email:

"I have always had a lot of respect for Bernie—his football intelligence and passion for football. I appreciate the support he has shown me through the years. I have always admired his preparation and commitment to the Browns—before, during and after Bill Belichick. I have enjoyed my communications with Bernie through the years."

It sounds very formal and sterile, but there is truth behind it. These guys now talk. They get along. They respect each other.

THE FALL OF BILL BELICHICK

"I know a lot of people don't think this looks like progress, but it is progress."

Bill Belichick told me that after the Browns' 1993 season, the year of Bernie Kosar being cut.

But the next season, with Vinny Testaverde as the starting quarterback and the importing of several players who were in New York when Belichick was an assistant coach with the Giants, the Browns finished 11-5. The key acquisitions were linebackers Carl Banks and Pepper Johnson.

They even knocked off New England in a playoff game before ending the 1994 post-season with a loss in Pittsburgh.

In some ways, it was a vindication for Belichick. Testaverde was a better quarterback than Kosar at this stage of their careers. Kosar had moved on to Miami, where he was a backup for the final three years of his career.

The 1994-95 coaching staff included Nick Saban, Kirk Ferentz, Eric Mangini, Jim Schwartz and Pat Hill. Saban, Ferentz and Hill became head coaches in college. Mangini, Schwartz and Saban also were head coaches in the NFL.

In the front office were future NFL general managers Ozzie Newsome, Phil Savage, George Kokinis, Mike Lombardi and Scott Pioli.

All were young men. Who knew Saban would become a Hall of Fame-caliber coach for Alabama? Or Newsome was destined to be one of the NFL's great executives? Or Ferentz would be a big-time coach at Iowa, or Pioli would help Belichick build some Super Bowl winners in New England?

And who knew Belichick would indeed turn into this generation's Paul Brown, a vision Art Modell had when hiring Belichick at the age of 38?

One theory is that if the team hadn't moved to Baltimore after the 1995 season, it was destined for a run that Belichick imagined in my 1993 interview: "My plan is for us to become a machine churning out good players for the next 7-8 years. My goal is to make us a good team every year."

After the 1994 season, it appeared the Browns took several significant steps down that road.

* * *

Belichick supporters point out the team was 4-5 when Modell gave a press conference on Nov. 6, 1995, explaining he would be moving the franchise to Baltimore after the season.

Following Modell's announcement, they were 1-6.

But even before that, the Browns and Belichick were having problems.

Belichick had also clashed often with his defensive coordinator, Nick Saban. Belichick, a former defensive coordinator, sometimes fell into the trap of doing his old job while doing his new job as head coach. Saban grew weary of the meddling. When Saban left the Browns to become head coach of Michigan State before the 1995 season, Belichick took over as defensive coordinator.

In 1995, the Browns' media guide listed Rick Venturi as the defensive coordinator, but Belichick made the big decisions on defense.

The Browns opened the season at 3-1.

Then they lost three games in a row. Testaverde was the quarterback during the three-game losing streak, and Belichick's faith in him was failing.

Belichick benched Testaverde, turning to rookie Eric Zeier, a third-round draft pick. The 3-4 Browns then beat Cincinnati 29-26 in overtime.

Zeier started the next three games, all losses.

Belichick returned to starting Testaverde. In some ways, this was a repeat of 1993 when the coach couldn't stick with a quarterback.

The owner gave a press conference in Baltimore about moving the team. Modell then stepped out of the public eye. He left Belichick to suffer the wrath of the media and fans. Games were ugly with booing chants of "BILL MUST GO" and "JUMP ART JUMP."

His disrespect and disdain for the media since being hired in 1991 made things even worse. The Kosar decision still hung over the franchise. A coach with a decent personality and a degree of public patience could have become a sympathetic figure.

* * *

One of coach Bill Belichick's biggest problems was general manager Bill Belichick. Modell had given Belichick full power over the organization.

Despite having lots of young talent in the front office, Belichick was making the draft picks. Those other front office people were like Belichick, very inexperienced in the area of the draft and player personnel.

As Ian O'Connor wrote in his 2018 biography of Belichick: "Belichick drafted 41 college players for the Browns and 40 of them failed to make even one Pro Bowl during their careers. The Browns often held early desirable picks in each round thanks to their losing records, and yet Belichick and Mike Lombardi failed to convert them into championship level depth."

Nor was Belichick's drafting improving over the years.

As O'Connor also noted: "Their six drafted players in 1995 started a combined 24 NFL games in their careers. Georgia quarterback Eric Zeier accounted for half of that total, and he went 4-8 as a starter."

Belichick's first round picks: Eric Turner (1991), Tommy Vardell (1992), Steve Everitt (1993), Antonio Langham (1994) and Craig Powell (1995). Turner was Belichick's only Pro Bowl selection.

His plan to have at least three Pro Bowlers on each side of the ball never happened in Cleveland.

One of the keys to his later success in New England was that Belichick and his player personnel director Scott Pioli changed their drafting strategy. One of the moves was to put less value on pure physical gifts of players and put more emphasis on guys who were productive players in college.

* * *

Belichick was fired after the 1995 season and before the new Browns (now Ravens) started playing in Baltimore.

Belichick returned to Bill Parcells, the coach who had a major influence on him with the Giants before coming to Cleveland. Now the head coach for New England, Parcells hired Belichick as his defensive coordinator in 1996. When Parcells moved to the Jets in 1997, Belichick followed.

This had to be a humbling experience for Belichick. Parcells was a tough guy who could be brutal on his assistants. Belichick brought some of those negative personality traits to Cleveland.

"If you're going to have the kind of career Bill has had, you need a quarterback like Tom Brady," said Ernie Accorsi, the Browns GM who pushed for the hiring of Belichick in Cleveland. "But had he

Bill Belichick runs off the field after a loss to Houston in Nov. 1993. "A lot of people don't think this looks like progress, but it is progress," he said. *Scott Shaw / The Plain Dealer*

stayed with the Browns or gone with them to Baltimore, I believe he'd have had winning records."

Being fired and returning to Parcells forced Belichick to take a hard look at what he'd done in Cleveland. It paid off with six Super Bowl titles once he was hired as the head coach of New England in 2000.

"Going back to Parcells made Belichick better because Parcells is one of the greatest coaches of all time," said Accorsi. "He has a concept of how to be a head coach that's unique. I'm sure he told Bill, 'In Cleveland, you did this wrong . . . you did that wrong.' "

Accorsi paused.

"It had to be absolutely humbling for Bill," said Accorsi. "Parcells doesn't pull any punches. Bill could have gone to a lot of places as a defensive coordinator, but he went back to Parcells because he knew he'd learn more from working for Parcells."

Accorsi said at one point, Belichick told him, "I really screwed up in Cleveland." The coach didn't elaborate. Accorsi also said his leaving the Browns in 1992 didn't help Belichick, and he apologized to the coach for that.

But it also must be said Belichick was not going to allow Accorsi or anyone else to have full power as a general manager.

"Bill learned a lot in Cleveland," said Accorsi. "Then he got Tom Brady. That also changed everything for him."

TIM COUCH GOT A RAW DEAL BUT STILL LOVES THE BROWNS

I remember sitting at the Browns training facility on the day the team drafted Tim Couch.

I found my original newspaper story about the 1999 draft, when the quarterback from Kentucky was the No. 1 selection:

"This blue-eyed kid with the close cropped, light brown hair looks like Everyone's All-American. Even more importantly, he acts like it. Couch handled the questions with ease and grace. He didn't say anything that offended anyone, yet was sure to give answers that were sincere and somewhat informative."

Looking back, these two questions cross my mind:

1. What did Couch really know about coming to the Browns in 1999?

2. What did any of us really know about what it would be like for the Browns to return as an expansion team in 1999?

"He's so wholesome, basic and normal," Browns CEO Carmen Policy said on that day. "His only complaint is he didn't have enough time to spend on his bass boat."

That's because Couch was on owner Al Lerner's private jet, flying from Lexington, Kentucky, to New York for the national draft show. Then back on the jet, from New York to Cleveland to meet the media here.

It seemed the Browns knew what they were doing.

This was before the NFL had a rookie salary cap. Top picks often held out during financial negotiations, missing parts of training camp and even some regular-season games. That often led to a setback for the team and the player. More than a few rookie years were knocked off track by the old system.

Lerner and Policy knew Couch wanted to be the first pick in the draft. They told his agent that Couch had to agree to a contract prior to the official announcement of the first pick.

No deal, no being the top pick in the draft.

The Browns and Couch agreed on a 7-year, $48 million contract with a $12 million bonus. It sounds relatively modest now, but it was big money back then.

New team, new quarterback, new start.

That's what it was to be in Cleveland, where 53,000 fans not only bought season tickets, they also paid for the dreaded Personal Seat Licenses (PSLs).

One NFL executive explained the PSL concept to me this way: "Imagine going to a grocery store. You expect to pay money for the groceries, but they also charge you big bucks for the cart even before you know what they have in the store."

That once inspired me to write: "Browns fans are so hungry for football, you probably can charge them 50 bucks each to sit in an empty stadium and stare at an orange helmet on the 50-yard line."

* * *

I talked to Couch years later, not long after the Browns beat Pittsburgh in the first round of the playoffs after the 2020 season. Couch is a huge Browns fan. "I watched every game," he said. He was thrilled for his old team.

We talked about being drafted by the Browns.

"You are so elated to be picked first, it's surreal," said Couch. "You never think you'll be the first pick in the draft. Then once reality sets in, you realize, 'Oh man, I'm going to the worst team in the league!' "

At this point in the new franchise's brief existence, veteran center Jim Pyne was still being celebrated as the team's first pick in the expansion draft, which was held months before the college draft.

There was excitement around Chris Palmer, the new head coach, who had a solid track record of developing quarterbacks. (Although Palmer was the team's fifth choice to be the head coach. The others refused to interview, or turned down a job offer.)

In a candid moment during his second season as coach, Palmer admitted to me, "I would have preferred to be the guy who followed me. You really don't want to be the first coach of an expansion team."

That's because you have no chance.

Such would be the case for Couch and Palmer.

But on April 17, 1999, the Browns were selling a dream and a story.

Couch was the perfect pick because he liked a challenge. He was one of the greatest athletes in Kentucky high school history, the state's player of the year in football and basketball. He averaged 36 points a game for Leslie High. Couch's grandfather worked in the coal mines near his home town of Hyden, population 350 when Couch grew up there. His mother was a social worker, his father was a transportation director for Leslie County.

Couch could have gone to any major football power in the country, but he chose the University of Kentucky—his home state school. Until Couch arrived, when someone mentioned Kentucky football, most fans changed the subject by asking. "When does basketball practice start?"

Kentucky basketball coach Rick Pitino offered a scholarship in case Couch didn't want to play quarterback for the Wildcats.

But Couch wanted to make football matter in his home state. He did just that, delivering a winning record and a bowl appearance.

This attitude and performance appealed to Browns CEO Carmen Policy. He talked about how Couch wasn't afraid of a challenge. He knew how to build something from the bottom. He was ideal for an expansion team.

In an April 4, 1999 story, USA Today had this to say of Couch: "The ultra-competitiveness, combined with an almost-Brett Favre-like playmaking ability has for months left many NFL personnel men saying Couch is as good as (his) gaudy numbers."

There were also comparisons to Peyton Manning. Some Browns fans hoped Couch would be the expansion team's version of Bernie Kosar.

* * *

There was a frenzy over the Browns being back with the first pick in the draft. That included the new front office.

Along with several other teams, the Browns attended a workout with Couch. They came away underwhelmed. They liked him personally. They admired what he did at Kentucky, setting several SEC passing records. But they had some doubts about his arm strength. After the workout, Palmer suggested a new grip on the football for Couch to help his accuracy.

Then the Browns scheduled a private workout for Couch. On Al Lerner's jet to Lexington, along with the team owner, were Policy, Palmer, general manager Dwight Clark and others. Many others, including quarterback coach John Hufnagel.

Hufnagel had the job of breaking down every pass Couch threw of at least 10 yards in his final season at Kentucky. There were 46 of

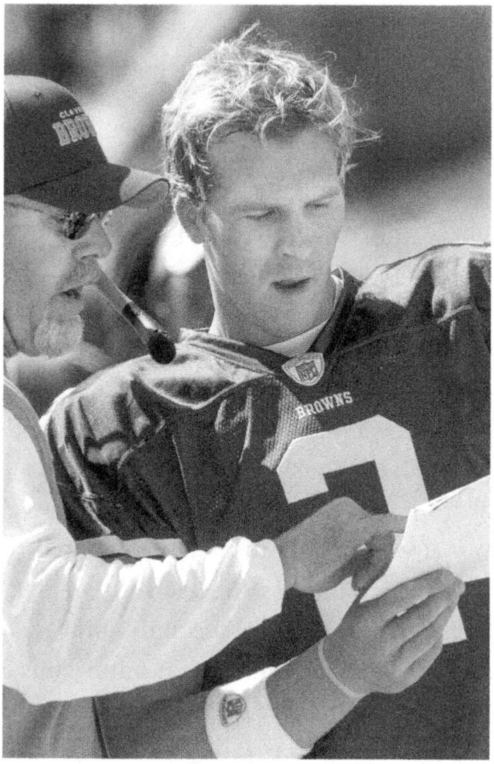

Tim Couch: "You never think you'll be the first pick in the draft. Then once reality sets in, you realize, 'Oh man, I'm going to the worst team in the league!'" *Chuck Crow / The Plain Dealer*

those throws, only three per game. That's because Kentucky used an early version of the no-huddle, fast paced "run-and-shoot" offense. That stressed quick short and medium passes. But the Browns thought Couch could play in a conventional offense.

The Browns sent a dozen people to the workout, "about everyone but the janitor," wrote Pat McManamon in the Akron Beacon Journal.

Couch had become close to Peyton Manning, the NFL's top draft pick in 1998. Manning told Couch of a private workout he had before the draft with the Colts, who then made him the No. 1 pick in the draft. He gave Couch some tips about how to handle it.

Couch handled it.

The Browns had him make 115 throws over 90 minutes.

"I put together big numbers in high school and college and it all came down to one workout," Couch said on draft night. "There was a lot of pressure in that workout, but it didn't bother me."

As they left Couch's workout, Palmer told Policy, "This is our guy."

Policy added, "And he's a solid human being."

On draft night, everyone was intoxicated with optimism.

Policy said Palmer "has Superman-type vision evaluating a quarterback."

Couch was used to being in the spotlight and hearing older adults gush, even embarrass themselves, when talking about him. His parents had instilled grace and humility in him, which served him well because the praise was outrageous for a 21-year-old going into an impossible expansion situation on that draft night.

"Tim Couch has always been the guy," said GM Dwight Clark. "He's always been the leader. He's always been the guy who rallied the troops. He was the best basketball player on his team. He set records in high school. He set records in college. We expect him to set records here."

* * *

The hype of draft night at the dawn of expansion football in Cleveland is almost invisible now in the rearview mirror of memory for most Browns fans.

But it had an impact on Couch, Palmer and the franchise.

The Browns could have taken Donovan McNabb or someone else. They would have been better off taking the trade offer from

New Orleans, which offered its entire set of draft picks for the top pick. But in the end, no matter who the Browns put on the field at quarterback in those early years, he was doomed for failure.

Let's revise that.

In those early years with the Browns, Tim Couch had no chance. When drafted, he was a sturdy, 6-foot-4, 220 pounds. But his career lasted only five seasons and 59 starts.

Consider this: You are starting an expansion team. You make a quarterback the top pick in your draft—No. 1 overall. What is the most important thing you can do to support the young quarterback, beyond good coaching?

That's right, a strong offensive line.

In the 1999 college draft, the Browns had 11 selections.

How many of those 11 were offensive linemen?

None. That's right . . . ZERO.

I never noticed this or heard it even mentioned back then. I only realized it when looking at the list of the Browns' 1999 draft picks when writing this book.

The Browns had five picks in the top 76 of the draft.

They took one quarterback (Couch), two defensive backs (Daylon McCutcheon and Marquis Smith), a receiver (Kevin Johnson) and a linebacker (Rahim Abdullah).

The Browns had taken a few linemen in the expansion draft, the best being veteran center Jim Pyne. They added a couple of other veterans via trade and free agency in David Wohlabaugh and Orlando Brown.

But the Browns threw together an offensive line much like they did everything else back then—without a lot of thought. Part of the problem was the 9-month frenzy between when the franchise was awarded to Cleveland and when the first game was to be played. It was the fastest start-up time for an NFL expansion franchise since the merger with the AFL in 1970.

But if you want to build a team to help your quarterback, you have to use at least one of those five picks in the first three rounds on a lineman. Someone has to block for the kid. Yes, Couch was legally an adult at 21 when drafted by the Browns, but he was a kid in terms of NFL experience and entering into a man's league with little pass protection.

As the season approached, I asked Palmer what was one of the biggest adjustments for Couch.

"The playbook," said the coach.

"What?" I asked.

"In college, Tim didn't have anything like the playbook we have here," he said. "They ran a very simple no-huddle offense. That stuff doesn't work in the NFL."

Palmer had a standard pro system with the quarterback often dropping back 5-to-7 steps and looking to throw medium and deep passes downfield. That also was new for Couch.

Dysfunction surfaced early. The front office of Policy and Clark had signed veteran Ty Detmer to start at quarterback. They wanted Couch to at least sit for several games, allowing him to learn the NFL.

Detmer started the opener, a home game against Pittsburgh. It was brutal. The Browns were behind 20-0 at the half. The offense was awful. Late in the fourth quarter, Palmer replaced Detmer with Couch. The Browns lost 43-0. They had nine yards rushing, 52 yards passing. They had just two first downs. That's right, TWO FIRST DOWNS!

Couch threw three passes, two incomplete and one intercepted.

Then Palmer announced Couch would start the next game.

Policy told me he was "shocked" by that news. It wasn't what they had discussed. But Palmer felt the best way to figure out how to play quarterback in the NFL was to play quarterback.

"The hardest part of being the face of a new franchise and the first pick in the draft was not winning games," said Couch. "It wears on you every week. The losses, they just pile up."

The Browns were 2-12 in games started by Couch. He was sacked a league-high 56 times.

"Some of the sacks were on me because I didn't get rid of the ball fast enough," he said. "Some were protection problems. Some were because we didn't have a lot of talent, being an expansion team."

* * *

By nature, Couch likes to do the right thing and please people.

"You feel the pressure," he said. "Or at least, I did. In almost every performance, you have to prove to people why you were selected before everyone else in the draft. You feel like you have to be perfect, and that's a terrible way to think."

But Couch also thought about how he defied the odds at Leslie High School and Kentucky, transforming both schools with his play on the football field.

"I'd never dealt with failure before the Browns," said Couch. "In high school, I was the No. 1 recruit in the country. In college, I was the SEC Player of the Year and a finalist for the Heisman Trophy. Then I got to the pros. I was losing games. I wasn't putting up numbers . . . You feel like you are letting people down."

Couch started the first seven games (2-5 record) of his second season, then broke his thumb in practice. He threw a pass, his arm came down after releasing the football and hit the helmet of a teammate.

Fracture. End of season.

In his third year (2001), Butch Davis was the coach. Couch started all 16 games, and the Browns were a respectable 7-9. Couch was sacked 51 times, second most in the NFL.

Couch was making progress, and so were the Browns. In 2002, the Browns finished 9-7. They made the playoffs, Couch having an 8-6 record as a starter.

"We played the final game of the regular season needing to beat Atlanta to make the playoffs," said Couch. "In the third quarter, I got hit and broke my leg. Kelly Holcomb came in and finished. We won, made the playoffs . . . but I couldn't play."

The Browns lost that postseason game 36-33 to Pittsburgh. Holcomb was brilliant, completing 26-of-43 passes for 429 yards and three touchdowns.

That performance led Butch Davis to name Holcomb the opening day starter in 2003. He did that based on "a gut feeling."

But Holcomb broke his leg that season. Couch played in 10 games, and he also was hurt. The Browns finished the 2003 season at 5-11.

Couch never played another NFL game after that.

"By 2003, I was already dealing with a lot of injuries," said Couch.

I asked Couch to list them:

Two shoulder surgeries.

A broken leg.

A broken thumb.

Multiple broken ribs.

Several concussions.

Two torn rotator cuffs.

A torn labrum.

A torn bicep.

There were others, but those were the major physical problems. His NFL career was over at 26, although he tried out for a few teams after that.

"It was a tough situation," said Couch. "I was a young player thrown into a new team where I was the starter in the second

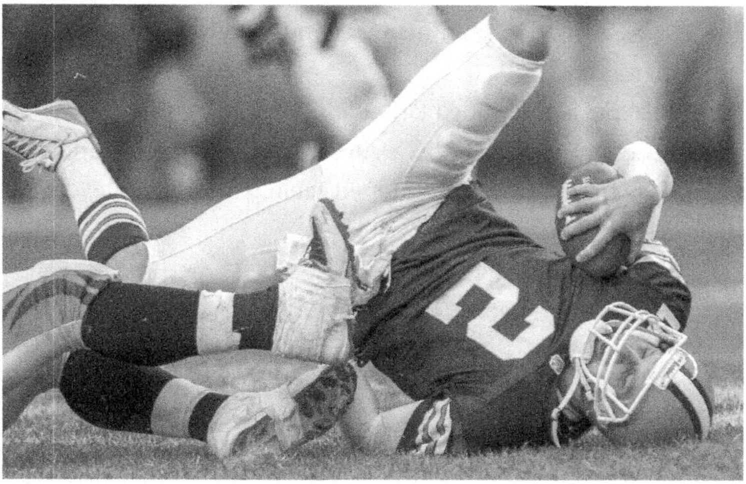

In the 1999 college draft, the Browns had 11 selections. How many were offensive linemen? None. By 2003, Couch was dealing with too many injuries to continue playing. *David I. Andersen / The Plain Dealer*

week of the season. I had some good games, but I couldn't sustain it. Once I'd start to build something, I'd get hurt."

Couch mentioned how NFL rules didn't protect quarterbacks in his era as they do now.

"We had some rugged defenses in our division," said Couch. "They'd just tee off on you."

* * *

It's unfair that Couch is considered a draft failure.

If you look at the third and fourth years of his career (2001-02) when the Browns finally had some talent and he stayed relatively healthy, the team had a 15-15 record with Couch as a starter.

He refused to make excuses about how the team didn't support him with a good offensive line. Palmer's offense also relied on deep throws, which led to more sacks and did not play to Couch's strength, which was short, quick passes.

Some fans might say, "I'm not feeling sorry for Couch, he made a ton of money."

That's true, something like $20 million in his career.

But Couch wanted to be a success for the Browns and their fans. Several times, he mentioned feeling "responsible" for the team's struggles.

He also paid a physical price.

In 2019, he had back fusion surgery.

"It was the worst surgery I've ever had," he said. "I was on a walker for two months. But it helped me so much. I'm not in pain anymore."

Couch doesn't know how many concussions he suffered. There were "several" in college and at least four in the NFL.

"They used to call it 'getting dinged' back then," he said. "It wasn't supposed to be a big deal."

People know better now.

"I'm pretty light sensitive, but that's not so bad. I can manage it. Given all I've been through, I'm in pretty good shape."

To this day, Couch says the Browns are his favorite team.

"I watch all their games," he said. "They gave me a chance to play in the NFL."

Couch occasionally wonders what would have happened if he had gone to an established team, as Ben Roethlisberger did when he joined the Steelers. He doesn't think he'd have been a great quarterback, but he probably could have had a long and successful career. That 15-15 record in 2001-02 was an indication of his ability.

"I'm proud of what I accomplished there," said Couch. "I wished I could have stayed healthier and played longer."

Couch has been delighted by the response of Browns fans when he meets them in person or on social media. He lives in Lexington, where he owns Meridian Wealth Management, a financial company, along with his brother, Greg Couch.

"It seems people now know when I was healthy, I was a pretty decent player," said Couch. "The fans have been great to me. They know I poured my heart and soul into that organization. I loved being a member of the Browns."

EVERY KICK COULD BE YOUR LAST: PHIL DAWSON

One of the things that makes Browns fans special is they know the value of kickers.

The team training facility in Berea is named after Lou Groza. Yes, he was a very good offensive tackle, but Groza is best known as a kicker.

"People in Cleveland have a healthy respect for kickers," said Phil Dawson. "You have Lou Groza in your storied history. Then other great kickers like Don Cockroft, Matt Bahr and Matt Stover. There have been a lot of incredible kickers in Cleveland, and the fans always showed their love to me."

It's why many Browns fans were outraged when after the 2012 season the Joe Banner front office decided not to re-sign Dawson. Dawson had been the team's kicker from the day they returned as an expansion team in 1999. He was an elite kicker, one capable of booting the football through the uprights in a blizzard on the shores of Lake Erie.

But Banner didn't think a kicker was worth $4 million—Dawson's previous salary and a rather modest sum in the overall payroll of an NFL team. Instead, he went with the cheaper Shayne Graham. When Graham didn't work out, Banner turned to Billy Cundiff.

Dawson signed with San Francisco for $2.2 million.

"The stereotype for pro kickers is you can find one on any street corner," said Dawson. "If that were true, why is there so much turnover in kickers when you only need 32 of them? And they can't even find 32 (to consistently do the job well)."

After Dawson, the Browns used nine different kickers between 2013-2020. Cody Parkey had two tours of duty.

"I still don't understand what the Browns did," said Dawson. "I established myself as a dependable guy and didn't show any signs of slowing down. I was kicking longer field goals as my career went on."

In 2012, at the age of 37, Dawson had perhaps the best season of his pro career. He was 29-of-31 on field goals, including perfect on seven attempts from 50 or more yards. In 2020, Parkey didn't even attempt a field goal from 50 or more yards.

Dawson kicked for six more seasons—four in San Francisco, two in Arizona. He signed a one-day contract with the Browns in 2019 so he could retire as an official member of the team. Of course, he never should have been told to leave.

* * *

Then again, Dawson almost didn't have an NFL career.

He was a record-setting kicker at the University of Texas, a two-time All-American.

"I had petitioned the NFL after my junior year to see what kind of interest there'd be if I turned pro," said Dawson. "They said I'd be a middle-round pick. I decided to go back to Texas for my senior year and had a good season."

Dawson heard that some NFL people said he might go as high as the second or third round in the 1998 draft. On draft day, he wanted to share the big moment when his name was called with his family.

"We rented my favorite barbecue joint in my home town of Dallas," said Dawson. "Back then, the first three rounds were on the first day. I didn't get picked. I thanked everyone, and said to stay tuned for tomorrow—that was when the rest of the rounds took place."

This time, the Dawson family invited people to their house. They had ESPN and Mel Kiper Jr. on the television. Day Two of the draft opened with the fourth round.

"We were sitting around, waiting for the phone to ring," said Dawson. "It never did."

Looking back 23 years, Dawson still can't believe it.

"I watched every pick," he said. "I was glued to the coverage. We had penciled in some teams we thought needed a kicker. When they got on the clock, we got excited. But once again, it wasn't me."

Not only that, no kicker or punter was picked in the 1998 draft.

"Those were the longest two days of my life," he said. "I had a big pro day. Lots of teams came. I went to the Senior Bowl. I kicked well. I had no indication the tide had turned against drafting me."

Dawson believes he was impacted because in 1997, the Packers had selected kicker Brett Conway in the third round, but he never played in a regular-season game for the Packers.

"Teams became afraid to draft kickers," Dawson said. "After the draft, I was rattled. You're told your whole life to just handle your business and things will take care of themselves. I felt like I did that. This was the first time in my life that statement was challenged."

After the draft, several teams called Dawson to try out.

He went to the old Three Rivers Stadium in Pittsburgh. It was springtime.

"There were no goal posts," said Dawson. "It was baseball season. Bill Cowher was the coach. He took me to the outfield

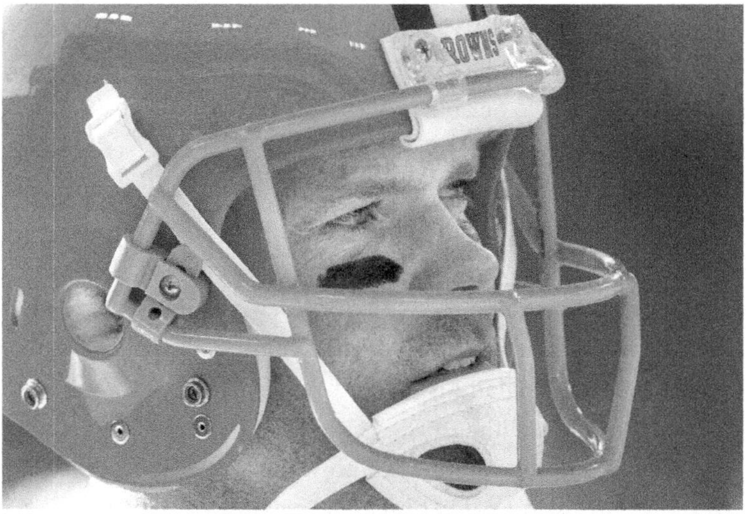

"I still don't understand what the Browns did," said Dawson. "I established myself as a dependable guy and didn't show any signs of slowing down. I was kicking longer field goals as my career went on." *Chuck Crow / The Plain Dealer*

and told me to aim in a certain direction. I was kicking with no uprights."

That didn't work.

"I found myself feeling a little intimidated," said Dawson. "There was some doubt. Maybe I wasn't as good as I thought I was."

He tried out for Oakland.

"The Raiders had the worst kicking performance in the NFL in 1997," said Dawson. "I made it through the minicamps. Once veteran camp started, it was clear I wasn't a good fit there. I asked for my release after the second preseason game and they were more than happy to grant it."

* * *

Dawson had never been cut from any team. In high school, he played linebacker on defense and offensive tackle on offense.

"I was severely undersized (5-foot-11, 200 pounds)," said

Dawson. "We ran the Wishbone offense and they need guys to stay low and chop-block people. I could do that. I had to learn every little detail to be able to stay on the field."

He also kicked. Then he went to Texas, where he set 13 school records by the time he turned pro. That's why he was shocked and shaken by the lack of interest from the NFL.

"In 1998, the Patriots claimed me on waivers," said Dawson. "I spent the entire season there on the practice squad. Adam Vinatieri was the kicker, and he was great with me. I learned so much from him. New England is where I first learned how to kick and handle the cold weather."

Dawson said he can now see how that 1998 season practicing with the Patriots prepared him for Cleveland.

"The Browns were an expansion team," said Dawson. "Vinatieri was a free agent. He was ready to go to Cleveland and sign. But at the last minute, he changed his mind and stayed in New England."

Then the Browns called Dawson.

"I went to Cleveland, Washington and Pittsburgh three days in a row to kick," said Dawson. "I admit, I still hadn't gotten over not being drafted . . . and being cut. But I chose to make that my motivation."

Dawson said when he worked out for the Browns it was February. They let him kick indoors in the field house. Browns Director of Football Operations Dwight Clark and special teams coach Ken Whisenhunt watched. Dawson said the Browns and Washington both offered him a contract. But the Browns "had a true opening because they were an expansion team."

When Dawson arrived at the first training camp for the new Browns in 1999, he was one of three kickers.

Remember, he had already been ignored in the draft, then let go by Oakland, Pittsburgh and New England.

"I never feared missing a kick," said Dawson. "Never struggled with confidence. But coming to the NFL was a foreign experience."

Dawson's first competition was with kickers Danny Kight and Jose Cortez. He outlasted them.

"But right at the end of training camp, they brought in Chris Boniol," said Dawson. "He had been a kicker with Dallas and the Eagles (for five seasons). Bringing in a veteran so late worried me. I thought I was doomed."

One day, Dawson saw Boniol packing up his stuff and leaving the locker room.

"I kept thinking this was my moment," he said. "I've been waiting for someone in the NFL to tell me, 'You're our guy.' "

Dawson saw Browns expansion head coach Chris Palmer walking down the hallway one way as he was heading the other.

Palmer stopped for a few seconds, then said, "Well, we're going to start with you."

Then Palmer walked away.

"That kind of reinforced all the uncertainty I was feeling," Dawson said. "I was thinking, 'I'm one missed kick or one bad game away from losing my job.' "

Dawson paused for a moment.

"For my next 21 years in the NFL, I don't think I ever got over that mentality completely," he said. "I remember that first year worrying if I'd have a job the next day. My wife (Shannon) deserves a medal for putting up with me."

* * *

In his rookie season with the Browns, Dawson connected on his first field goal attempt—a 41-yarder. He also drilled a 39-yarder as time expired giving those expansion Browns a 16-15 victory in Pittsburgh—where he finally was able to kick with the goal posts in place.

He also scored the first rushing TD in the history of the new franchise, a 4-yard scamper on a fake field goal.

Dawson was 8-of-12 in field goals as a rookie in 1999. By far, it was the worst season of his pro career until his final season in Arizona.

"What saved me that season was making that kick to beat Pittsburgh," he said. "But nothing was guaranteed. I was on a minimum contract. We rented an apartment with the shortest lease we could find. Some of the wives of the older players told my wife, 'Don't hang up any curtains. As soon as you put up curtains, you're gone.'"

Dawson paused.

"I think it was seven years before we finally put up curtains," he said. "In my 14 years in Cleveland, there were only 2-or-3 years where there wasn't another kicker in camp. I saw anyone they brought in as a threat. I don't know if I ever reached a point where I thought the other kicker was just a 'training camp guy.' I viewed him as someone who could take my job."

* * *

The weather makes Cleveland one of the hardest places to kick in the NFL.

"I had to figure out how to kick in Cleveland with the wind and the cold," he said. "Back then, there were only 30 jobs—not just in the NFL, but 30 kicking jobs like this in the world. You couldn't be picky. Don't complain about it."

He used to go to FirstEnergy Stadium during the week to practice kicking. "But I stopped after a few years. The weather on Wednesday was not the same as Sunday. It was always changing."

Dawson was like legendary Cleveland weatherman Dick Goddard in an orange helmet.

"I studied weather patterns," he said. "I was almost psycho

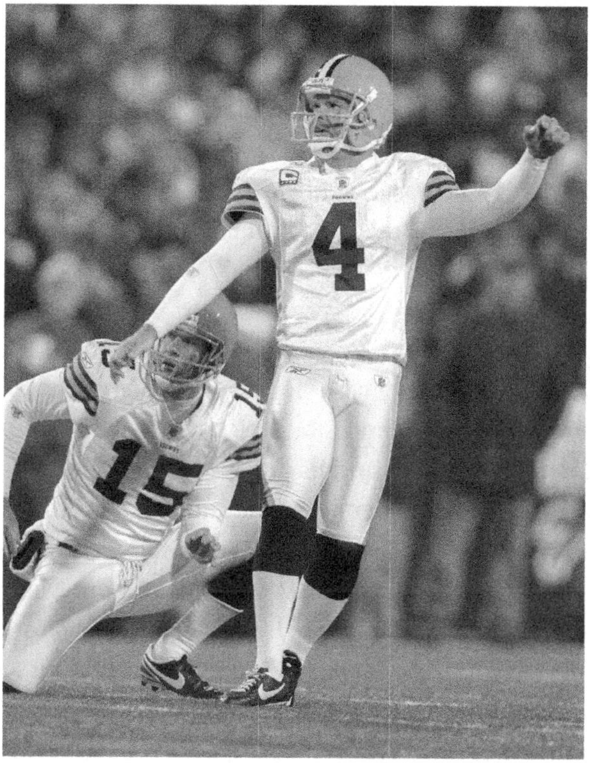

"I had to figure out how to kick in Cleveland with the wind and the cold. Back then, there were only 30 kicking jobs like this in the world. You couldn't be picky. Don't complain about it." *Chuck Crow / The Plain Dealer*

about that. I used weather.com because it was better with temperature and precipitation. But accuweather.com was better for wind velocity. I studied both."

Dawson said for every 10-degree drop in temperature, a kicker will often lose a yard or two in distance and a half-second in hang time.

"To be a kicker in Cleveland and survive, you have to be a good one," he said. "There's no just hanging around, being mediocre. The elements will quickly expose you. It's not like being in a dome or some warm weather cities where you can just go out and kick—fewer variables to worry about."

So he figured out how to kick in Cleveland?

"No way," he said. "You have to figure it out one kick at a time. There is the footing issue, bad weather can be a problem there. The winds change. There are so many calculations going into each kick."

* * *

Dawson makes the case for kickers being the loneliest, least-understood position in the NFL.

"If I'm a quarterback and having problems with my accuracy, there's going to be someone in the building (on the coaching staff) to help me with technique," said Dawson. "The same with all the other positions. But when you're a kicker and you're struggling, there's no one in-house to help you. Special teams coaches generally know zero about kicking. You have to fix yourself."

Dawson said a few teams are starting to add kicking coaches, but it's not a general practice across the NFL.

"About 95% of the time, it was me taking tapes home from practice and watching it myself," he said. "I had to figure it out. Just as I wouldn't complain about kicking in a hard environment, I couldn't complain about not having anyone on the coaching staff to help me."

Dawson said he can remember only two possible game-winning kicks that he missed while in Cleveland.

"No one feels worse about it than the kicker when he misses, especially that kind of important kick," said Dawson. "But to me, every kick was a big kick. I mean that. Because every kick could be your last kick."

Dawson had a special approach.

"Some people thought kickers just show up in practice, kick a few balls and go home," said Dawson. "I was the opposite. I was in the weight room with the guys. I went to meeting rooms with other position groups. I was watching tape like they do, grinding away. I stayed after practice."

That's true. Former Browns coach Pat Shurmur often said that of Dawson. Shurmur made Dawson a team captain. He would privately talk to Dawson about some issues on the team. Rarely is a kicker considered a team leader, but after a few years in Cleveland that was Dawson with the Browns.

"Because I worked so hard and was connected to the other players, that helped me when I had a rough patch," said Dawson. "I knew I had their support. Sometimes, they showed more confidence in me than I had in myself. So did the fans. I felt it. It allowed me to do things I didn't even think I could do."

* * *

Dawson never wanted to play anywhere but Cleveland.

"Devastating," he said. "That's how I felt at the end of 2012 when I became a free agent and I wasn't given an opportunity to remain a Brown. Why would I ever want to leave? I'd invested 14 years in Cleveland. I grew to love not only the team but the city, the fans—everything."

Dawson is now an assistant football coach at Lipscomb Academy in Nashville. The head coach is former Browns QB Trent Dilfer. Dawson loves working with high school kids, and likes the Christian-school setting. His son Beau is on the football team. He will be a senior in the fall and plays H-back and long-snapper.

"I loved everything about Cleveland," he said. "The fans. The team. I'll never forget and treasure it always."

DRAFTED FROM HIS BASEMENT: AARON SHEA

Aaron Shea never made a Pro Bowl. Most of his teams were losers, as he came to the Browns in the expansion era. When my friend and local radio personality Mark "Munch" Bishop suggested I interview Shea for a Plain Dealer story on players and draft day, I was lukewarm to the idea.

"He's a good guy," said Bishop. "You'll like him."

I looked up Shea's career. He was in the NFL for six seasons, all with the Browns. He started 30 games, played in 65 as a tight end and an occasional fullback. He covered kickoffs and punts on special teams.

Then I thought of something Joe Thomas once mentioned when talking about his under-appreciated teammates. He called them "working class" and "middle class" veterans, meaning they battled to make the roster in the first place and fought to stay in the league.

Shea was one of those guys.

* * *

On the day he was drafted by the Browns, Aaron Shea was hiding in his basement.

"This was 2000," said Shea. "The first three rounds of the draft were on Saturday. I watched it on TV. I was like a little kid, waiting for (ESPN's) Mel Kiper to talk about me being picked."

But no one called his name.

Shea had been a fullback and tight end at Michigan, an honorable mention All-Big Ten selection along with teammate Tom Brady.

"I was getting calls from Miami, Denver and the Chargers," said Shea.

The phone would ring. He'd answer, believing a team had drafted him.

"Instead, they'd say things like, 'Hang in there' as if they were getting ready to take me," said Shea. "Miami flew me down for a visit. They said if I was still available in the third round, they'd take me."

He was available.

"Miami took a defensive back (Ben Kelly) instead," said Shea.

So ended the opening day of the 2000 draft for Shea and his family in rural Ottawa, Illinois.

Then Day 2 of the draft opened. It rained. And rained. The wind whipped, the power went out while a tornado warning was in effect near the Shea homestead.

"We headed to the basement," he said. "No TV. I'm waiting to hear I was drafted, and I couldn't even watch. I was still getting calls from teams that hadn't drafted me."

* * *

One call was different. Shea noticed a 440 area code on the caller ID. He had no idea where that would be from.

He answered, and someone asked him, "How do you like the state of Ohio?"

Shea thought it was another dumb call. He said, "I'm not a big fan."

The voice said, "Oh, that's right. The Ohio State/Michigan thing. Well, how do you like Cleveland?"

"Actually, I like Cleveland," said Shea.

Then Chris Palmer got on the phone and the Browns coach welcomed Shea to the team. He was their fourth-round pick, No. 110 overall.

Shea laughs as he tells the story. When his father saw Shea having a longer-than-normal draft day conversation on the phone, he asked his son, "Is it Denver?"

"Dad," said Shea. "Please shut up!"

To this day, Shea still isn't sure who made the initial call from Browns headquarters in Berea.

"It wasn't (GM) Dwight Clark and it wasn't Coach Palmer," said Shea. "Maybe it was a scout."

Shea was telling the truth about not being a big Ohio fan but having kind thoughts about his new team and city.

"I went to the first Browns game in 1999," said Shea.

Why?

Shea said he and Michigan quarterback Tom Brady were friends with Pat Kratus, a Michigan teammate from St. Ignatius. He wanted to see the new Browns play. They figured out how to get tickets and off they went.

"We ended up sitting in a suite," said Shea. "The Browns got killed, but we had a great time. And I really did like Cleveland."

The Browns lost to Pittsburgh that night, 43-0.

"After I hung up talking to Coach Palmer, I realized I was going to the team that I saw that day, the team that won two games all year," said Shea. "That was coming from Michigan back when we won all the time."

Shea even watched some of the Browns games in that 1999 expansion season when they were 2-14. If nothing else, seeing the lack of talent on the field gave him confidence he'd make the team.

Aaron Shea in 2004. On draft day, the Michigan grad answered the phone and someone asked, "How do you like the state of Ohio?" "I'm not a big fan," he replied. But he played—and stayed. *Chuck Crow / The Plain Dealer*

Not long after being drafted by the Browns, he received a call from former Michigan coach Lloyd Carr.

"You be humble in victory," Carr told his player, soon to be a pro.

"What do you mean, Coach?" Shea asked.

"You be humble in victory," Carr repeated.

Once Shea joined the Browns, he understood what Carr meant. He was no longer a prize recruit. He was going into the NFL, where coaches were quickly fired, players often cut.

* * *

Shea received a $276,000 signing bonus and a salary of $174,000 for the 2000 season.

"I never had money in college," said Shea. "It was hard to scrape together $20. So I put my entire signing bonus in my checking account. Then I took out a bunch of friends and said, 'I got drinks tonight!' "

Nothing besides his signing bonus and first year salary was guaranteed, even though his contract was for four years.

Shea later hired a financial advisor and quickly got that money out of the checking account and into some safe investments.

"I got into a fight in my first week of practice," said Shea.

The Browns had two tight ends from Michigan, the other being Mark Campbell. He signed with the Browns as an undrafted free agent in the 1999 expansion year. He also was one of the players Shea and Brady visited after watching the Browns being smashed by the Steelers in that first game. The Browns were 3-13 in his first season. Shea played in all but one game, starting eight and catching 30 passes. That would be the most receptions of any season in his NFL career.

"I was playing with some people who told me, 'Win or lose, you get a paycheck on Wednesday,' " said Shea. "I came from Michigan with Coach Carr. We didn't accept losing. That attitude bothered me."

In his four years at Michigan, Shea's teams had a 40-9 record. They lost only five games in his final three seasons.

The Browns were 3-13 in Shea's rookie season.

* * *

Shea quickly became close to Tim Couch, and watched as the quarterback consistently was sacked and injured. Couch was on a bad team behind a poor line. Shea began a relationship with Chris Palmer, and then the coach was fired after the 2000 season.

"I think Chris Palmer could have been a great coach if they gave him a chance," said Shea. "And Tim (Couch) would have played well for 10 years in the NFL if they had taken care of him. He got a raw deal."

Shea's career lasted six years. Couch only played five.

Right after Couch was forced to retire because of various injuries, he had this conversation with Shea.

"I was a fourth-round pick and you were the No. 1 pick in the (1999) draft," said Shea.

"But you're still playing," said Couch.

"How about this?" asked Shea. "Let's switch bank accounts, and you can keep playing."

"No, I'm good," said Couch.

Yes, Couch was paid well. He also was done as a player at the age of 26—and missed the game dearly.

* * *

Shea had a strong early career, then injuries hit. One shoulder problem after another. A bad ankle. A cranky back.

"I've had three shoulder surgeries and a torn bicep," he said. "I had back problems near the end of my career."

Players like Shea list their injuries with an impersonal, almost robotic voice. You don't hear the pain. You don't feel his frustration. You don't even come close to having an idea what it means to have your pro football dream over before the age of 30—as Shea did.

Think about it . . .

Three shoulder surgeries, each time thinking this operation will fix it and be the last.

A torn bicep, more surgery.

"Then I developed back trouble in my last year," he said. "I still have it. Once it starts, it seems to never end . . . I went to doctors in

Cleveland, on the East Coast and on the West Coast. None of them thought any surgery could get it right. It's just a weird injury."

* * *

Shea dismissed the complaints of a few former Michigan players who were with the Browns and thought fans were tough on them because they had been Wolverines.

"You play hard, the fans will appreciate you," said Shea. "They don't care if you're from Michigan. Steve Everitt (a former Michigan player with the Browns 1993-95) told me that. He was right."

After retiring from football because of all the injuries, Shea worked for the Browns for several seasons. He now works for a title company and does some investment banking. He married a woman from Westlake, and settled in the West Side suburb.

Some of Shea's former Michigan teammates have said, "Of all the guys who stayed in Ohio, it's YOU!"

"I married someone from here," he said.

"But you're a Michigan man," they said.

"I get it," said Shea. "But there is good and bad everywhere you go. Cleveland is a great sports town. They love football."

Then he mentions something else.

"I was with the Browns longer (six years) than I was with Michigan," he said. "This place is special to me."

BE CAREFUL WHAT YOU WISH FOR: BRADY QUINN

Be careful what you wish for?

That is part of the Brady Quinn story. When the Browns found a way to draft the Notre Dame quarterback in 2007, Quinn was sure Cleveland was the right place to be.

The Browns worked hard to obtain Quinn, trading their 2007 second round pick and their 2008 first round selection to Dallas for the 22nd pick in the 2007 draft.

That became Quinn.

"I thought it was more than an opportunity, it was destiny," recalled Quinn.

Quinn was a kid from Dublin, Ohio, near Columbus, who had a Browns poster on his wall. It was a picture of Cleveland Stadium with a headline proclaiming: WELCOME BRADY QUINN!

"I had that in my room from the time I was 5 years old," said Quinn.

Some fans will recall watching the 2007 draft. Quinn remembered about eight players showing up in New York for the event, all of them expected to be selected near the top.

And Quinn?

There was a debate about him being the first-or-second best quarterback, the other option being LSU's JaMarcus Russell.

When Oakland opened the draft by grabbing Russell, Detroit had the next pick. The Lions went with Calvin Johnson, a future Hall of Fame receiver.

"The question you have to ask yourself if you're a Detroit Lions fan is 'Why not a quarterback? Why not Brady Quinn?' " said ESPN draft expert Mel Kiper immediately after the selection was made.

The Browns were at No. 3. They finished the 2006 season with a 4-12 record. Charlie Frye and Derek Anderson were their starting quarterbacks. Quinn had set several passing records at Notre Dame. He was a great college player, period.

The Browns needed a quarterback. Quinn was rated among the top two in the draft. He also wanted to play for the Browns.

"I had a visit with them in Berea and it was awesome," said Quinn. "I watched film and went over Xs and Os with (offensive coordinator) Rob Chudzinski. Then I met (coach) Romeo Crennel, and he was great. I was really excited about the Browns."

Quinn's highest praise was for general manager Phil Savage.

"He was one of the most genuine people I met during the draft process," he remembered. "I kept thinking it would be great to play for the Browns—and I sensed they were sincerely interested in me."

* * *

Before looking at what happened to Quinn with the Browns, Quinn's pre-draft experience is fascinating to consider. Quinn had reason to believe he'd be at least a top 10 pick. Most of the teams drafting high visited with him in person.

But some of those meetings were, well . . . odd.

"I went to Oakland and met with (coach) Lane Kiffin," said Quinn. "Lane told me, 'We'd love to have you, but we're taking the other guy.' "

Kiffin meant Russell.

Quinn also met with Al Davis, the legendary owner of the Raiders.

"He seemed most interested in looking at the different colors of silver they were using on the helmets," said Quinn. "But it was cool to meet someone who was such a part of NFL history."

Nonetheless, Quinn had to wonder, "Why am I here?"

He went to Detroit and met with their coaching staff. Tampa Bay coach Jon Gruden traveled to the Notre Dame campus in South Bend to have dinner with Quinn. They also worked him out throwing to Bucs receivers Maurice Stovall and Michael Clayton.

The Bucs had finished 4-12. Their starting quarterback was Bruce Gradkowski. So they seemed a serious possibility to take him with the No. 4 pick.

* * *

Quinn also visited Washington, which had the No. 6 pick.

"I remember walking into the weight room and seeing Mark Brunell on the treadmill, staring at me," said Quinn.

Brunell was the team's starting quarterback in 2006. Washington also had Jason Campbell. Neither was thrilled to spot their possible replacement.

Quinn talked to coach Joe Gibbs, offensive coordinator Al Saunders and defensive coordinator Gregg Williams. He enjoyed the conversations, but once again he was wondering, "Why am I here?"

Then he met Washington owner Dan Snyder, and the Washington coaches urged Quinn to tell their boss why he had decided to do the bench press drill at the NFL Combine.

Quinn had been dealing with a minor injury and didn't throw at the Combine. His agent Tom Condon and Notre Dame coach Charlie Weis told him not to lift weights at the event. Take it easy and get healthy for his upcoming pro day.

But a few NFL scouts at the Combine convinced Quinn to do the bench press—which he did. He set an NFL Combine record for quarterbacks by bench-pressing 225 pounds 24 times. He had more reps than star linebacker Patrick Willis, who had 22.

"Coach Weis let me have it in language that was, let's say, very colorful," said Quinn. "My agent also said I was wrong to do it, but he didn't use the same language as Coach Weis."

The coaches roared as Quinn told the story, which also amused Snyder.

"I think that was the only reason they brought me to Washington," said Quinn.

* * *

Quinn also met with Minnesota and Miami.

Adding it up, he had visits with seven of the top nine teams picking in the NFL draft.

"I wouldn't get past Miami at No. 9," said Quinn. "I had a meeting with (coach) Cam Cameron and (assistant) Terry Robiskie."

In 2006, the Dolphins were 6-10. Their starting quarterback was Joey Harrington. They needed help at Quinn's position.

A few days before the draft, a package arrived at the Notre Dame football office of Charlie Weis.

"The Dolphins sent him a bunch of stuff (hats, shirts, etc.)," said Quinn. "Coach Weis called and told me about it. It seemed like Miami wanted me."

* * *

The night before the draft, Savage called Tom Condon, Quinn's agent.

"We really like Brady," said Savage. "But if Joe Thomas is there, we are taking him at No. 3. I'm telling you this because I know how much Brady wants to be a Brown and I don't want him to be disappointed."

Condon called Quinn, repeating the message from Savage.

"I don't know if this is a smoke screen or what," said the agent. "I've never had a call like this the night before the draft. I wanted you to know about it."

Because Quinn left Berea with such a positive impression of Savage, he believed the GM was telling the truth.

Savage once told me the Browns had a vigorous internal debate about Thomas vs. Quinn at No. 3. Offensive coordinator Rob Chudzinski pushed hard for Quinn.

Savage believed Thomas had a chance to be a great left tackle, and he couldn't pass on that. But in the back of his mind, he was considering ways to also trade back into the first round and take Quinn if the quarterback slipped out of the top 10.

* * *

Quinn brought several members of his family with him from Ohio to the draft in New York.

"I know some guys stayed home," he said. "But this was something great for our family. Some of them had never been to New York and would never go to New York again."

Quinn wore a sharp suit. The crew from Columbus assumed their favorite player would soon have his name called. After all, he set 36 school records and was a first-or-second-team All-American selection for several media outlets.

Oakland took Russell. Detroit took Calvin Johnson, surprising draft guru Mel Kiper. The Browns kept their word and selected Joe Thomas, who was at the time fishing on Lake Michigan with family, their idea of a draft day party.

Other names were called: Gaines Adams, Levi Brown, LaRon Landry, Adrian Peterson and Jamaal Anderson.

"It was Miami's turn," said Quinn. "I thought this was it, they were going to take me."

During the draft, the cameras had focused on Quinn and his family, the discouragement bubbling up with each team calling out someone else's name.

At No. 9, Miami selected Ted Ginn Jr., the receiver from Glenville High and Ohio State.

"When that happened, I knew I was in trouble," said Quinn. "Most teams coming after them didn't need a quarterback."

* * *

Soon, Quinn and his family were alone in the Green Room. All the other players in New York had been picked.

"After the top 10, I was hungry and I had to go to the bathroom," said Quinn. "I finally got up and left."

Some of Quinn's friends and family went out for food. They came back with Chipotle.

Commissioner Roger Goodell eventually took Quinn and his family out of the Green Room and away from the cameras.

"Playing at Notre Dame, I was used to being in the public eye," said Quinn. "My family wasn't. It was hard with the cameras on them. They didn't sign up for this."

The hours passed by . . . as in four hours since the start of the draft. Then Quinn received a call from Fox Sports reporter Jay Glazer.

"Baltimore is trying to trade up to 23 to get you," Glazer said.

Quinn got excited. Baltimore. GM Ozzie Newsome, a former Brown. A good organization. Could play the Browns twice a year. Yes, Baltimore could be good. It would be fun to beat the Browns after they passed on him.

Quinn spent about 10 minutes on the phone talking to Newsome and others with the Ravens.

"I was ready to go to Baltimore," said Quinn.

Then the phone rang. It wasn't Baltimore.

With about two minutes left before the 22nd pick was to be made, Quinn's phone rang. The incoming call had a 216 area code.

"Cleveland," thought Quinn.

It was Ryan Seelbach, a member of the Browns front office. He said Cleveland had made a deal with Dallas for the 22nd pick, and Quinn was now a Brown.

"I was grabbing my jacket and someone was putting a Browns cap on my head," said Quinn. "They were leading me out to the stage. I felt like I was watching myself in a movie, hovering over everything."

The Browns had traded their second-round pick in 2007 and a first rounder in 2008 to the Cowboys for the 22nd pick and a chance to draft Quinn.

"I kept thinking about how I wanted to play for the Browns and it looked like it wouldn't happen—then it did," said Quinn. "It felt like destiny. It felt like my life had prepared me for this."

Savage was overjoyed with the picks of Joe Thomas and Quinn.

"This will probably be the day that defines the Browns' turnaround, if indeed it does happen," Savage said. "If we are going to do it, this is one of those stepping stone days."

Savage talked about how he had been trying to trade up to draft Quinn starting at No. 12, and how he never believed the quarterback would drop to number 22.

Maybe . . . just maybe . . . the Browns had found their quarterback.

* * *

Quinn missed the start of training camp because of a brief contract negotiation holdout, but the Browns had already decided they'd open the 2007 season with Derek Anderson or Charlie Frye at quarterback. They didn't want to have Quinn start early in the season.

But they also thought at some point, Quinn would take over as the starter.

Frye started the opener but was benched late in the second quarter in favor of Anderson. Anderson went on to have a career year, leading the Browns to a 10-6 record. Quinn threw only eight passes that entire season. In 2007, Anderson was a good starting quarterback for a winning team in Cleveland. But that winning season was like a comet streaking across the sky—here and gone. In 2008, Anderson started, was benched. Then Quinn took over. He got hurt. Anderson came back. He got hurt. The Browns went through four different starting quarterbacks.

They finished 4-12 in 2008. Savage and the coaching staff were fired.

* * *

Looking back, Quinn was overrated coming out of Notre Dame. But Savage and some others still believe he could have been a solid starter in the right system.

"A quarterback needs a sponsor, someone who can get the organization to believe in him," said Savage. "After I was fired, Brady lost that."

Eric Mangini became head coach in 2009. He didn't like Anderson or Quinn. He kept switching quarterbacks. Quinn also suffered some more injuries. Then he was traded to Denver.

By 2010, Quinn had gone from a promising quarterback prospect to a guy trying to keep a job as a backup.

"In 2008, I got a chance to play, but broke my right index finger and had two pins put in," said Quinn. "I tried to play with it, but I could hardly grip the ball."

The reason Denver traded for Quinn in March 2010 was

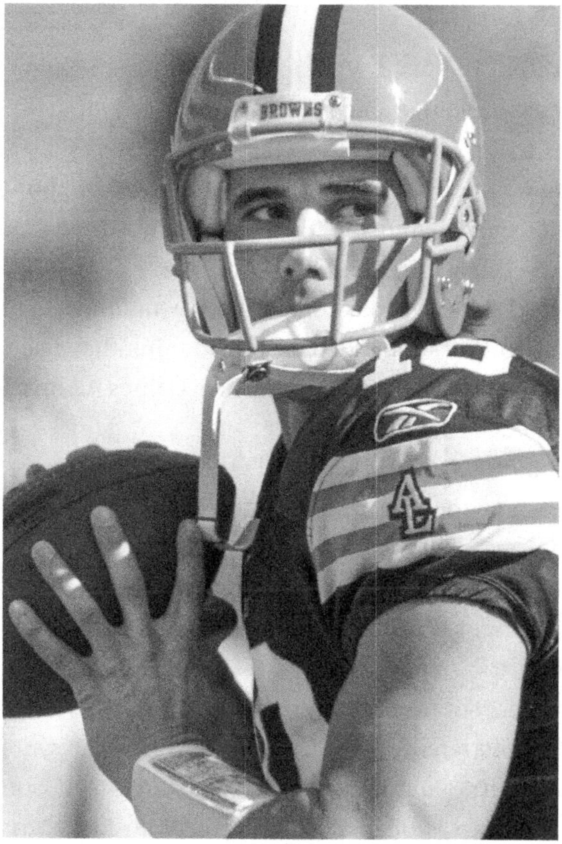

The Browns front office believed Brady Quinn would be a solid starter in the right system. But they didn't provide him with much stability. *Chuck Crow / The Plain Dealer*

because coach Josh McDaniels liked him. But 12 games into the 2010 season, McDaniels was fired.

Quinn later went to Kansas City and started eight games for a bad team in 2012. He had two major concussions. He had a significant back surgery. He bounced from New England to the Jets to Miami before retiring in 2014. He started 20 NFL games in his 7-year career.

* * *

What were ESPN's draft experts saying about Quinn in 2007? Here is an exchange between Todd McShay and Kiper about picks No. 2 (Detroit) and No. 3 (Cleveland):

McShay: "I know this will drive their fans crazy, but the Lions will select Calvin Johnson. They should take Brady Quinn, but you get the sense they don't like him."

Kiper: "If the Lions pass on Quinn, it would be yet another in a long line of questionable decisions. I think they will, although not for Johnson. They'll take Clemson's Gaines Adams, a Simeon Rice-type edge rusher."

Then they discussed Cleveland's pick:

Kiper: "For the same reasons the Lions should take Quinn, Cleveland actually will. They need a franchise face."

McShay: "When you can draft a franchise QB, you do it. People say Quinn can't win the big game. They said that about Peyton (Manning), too."

There were some warning signs.

Sports Illustrated's Peter King wrote this about Quinn before the 2007 draft: "Quinn couldn't win the big one at Notre Dame, wasn't accurate enough and had 3-4 brain-locked passes per game."

King also wrote: "For much of the year, Quinn had been the odds-on favorite to be the draft's first pick. But he played poorly in bad losses to highly ranked Michigan and USC . . . When Notre Dame and LSU squared off in the Sugar Bowl . . . LSU rolled 41-14. Quinn was chased all over the Superdome for four quarters, looked jittery and struggled (15-for-35, 148 yards, two TDs, two interceptions)."

Quoted in the same story, in King's discussion of JaMarcus Russell vs. Quinn for the first pick, was Cleveland's Phil Savage: "The repercussions of this pick will last for years. You're picking a flavor. Brady is probably the safer pick. He's been so well-schooled in every aspect of quarterback play, and we've had four years to evaluate him because he's played so much college football."

Russell went to Oakland at the top of the draft. His career lasted three seasons. He had a 7-18 record as a starter. Russell had a lot of personal problems and ranks as one of the worst No. 1 picks in NFL history.

The entire 2007 draft was a disaster for quarterbacks. ESPN's Mark Simon wrote an in-depth story about it in 2017, pointing out that only one QB (Trent Edwards) won 10 games as a starter. Quinn had a 4-16 record as a starter.

* * *

In some ways, quarterbacks are like restaurants. Part of their success is due to location, another part to management.

What if Brady Quinn had ended up with Baltimore, a winning and stable organization?

"I think about that once in a while," said Quinn. "I saw what Joe (Flacco) did there. Maybe it would have been different for me."

Savage believes Quinn could have been a viable NFL starting quarterback in a different place—or even if Savage had remained in Cleveland after the 2008 season.

"We could have built a team around Brady to help him," said Savage. "We would have been committed to finding out if he could play. He needed support and patience."

But front office and coaching changes didn't lead to either happening for Quinn.

Meanwhile, Baltimore drafted Joe Flacco with pick No. 18 in 2008. The Ravens committed to him. Never a flashy player, Flacco was mostly solid. He started 11 years in Baltimore with a 96-67 record.

Could that have been Quinn if the Browns had passed on him in the 2007 draft? Who knows? But his odds of NFL success would have been dramatically higher with that organization.

Quinn has recreated himself with Fox Sports doing NFL and college games. He also does talk radio. He's a natural in the media.

"I remember calling five NFL games in 2014 right after Miami let me go," he said. "I enjoyed it, but kept thinking I should be down there—playing. I missed it. But I'm grateful I got to play. I'm still a Browns fan. I got really excited watching them make the playoffs (in 2020). They're still my team."

THE MOST UNDERRATED BROWN

When he was receiving his COVID-19 vaccination shot, the elderly man wore a mask reading Cleveland Browns Alumni. This was in St. Augustine, Florida.

A woman was staring at him. She finally asked, "Why do you have that on?"

"What are you talking about?" asked the man.

"The mask," she said.

"I just happened to have played for the Cleveland Browns," he said.

Then he introduced himself as Ernie Green.

"OH, MY!" she squealed.

She said she was the president of the Browns Backers in Jacksonville, Florida.

"We have 125 members," she said. "We'd love to have you join us and be a part of that."

It wasn't clear if the woman knew a lot about Ernie Green. The fact that he once played for the Browns was enough. Most Browns fans have at least heard the name at some point, probably in connection with the 1964 championship Browns. But very few fans know much about Ernie Green, who is one of my all-time favorite Cleveland Browns.

* * *

Ernie Green grew up in the Jim Crow South of the 1940s and 1950s. There were plenty of "separate" facilities, but very few were equal for the African-Americans of that era.

He was a star running back for Spencer High in Columbus, Georgia. He was president of his senior class, a member of the National Honor Society—a true "student athlete." Today, he'd be a top recruit of Georgia, Alabama and other SEC schools. Not back then. Not the era of "No Colored Allowed" and "Whites Only" signs on some doors. In other places, such as those deep South football programs, those words were also in the hearts and minds of the coaches.

"I heard from a lot of the Black colleges like Clark, Morehouse and Morris Brown," said Green. "Most people thought I'd go to a place like Florida A&M. But Louisville had recruited a running back from Birmingham who played well for them. He was about to graduate, and they were looking for a replacement."

Louisville coach Frank Camp called several coaches at primarily black southern high schools and heard about Green. That led to a scholarship offer from Louisville—sort of. It was a bus ticket.

For 12 hours, Green sat on a bus going to a new city. It was a long, lonely ride. When he arrived at the bus station in Louisville, there was no one from the college to greet him. He was about to catch a bus back home when he remembered having a slip of paper with the coach's name on it—Frank Camp. Green then found a phone book. Sure enough, Camp was listed. He called the coach, who sent someone to pick up the new recruit.

Actually, this was a tryout for a scholarship. Louisville had a back named Lenny Lyles who broke the racial color line on the football team in 1954. He was headed to the Baltimore Colts. The coaches had Green race Lyles. It was close, but Lyles won. Then they had Green take part in a few pass catching drills.

Finally, they offered him a scholarship and $15 a month laundry money. Part of Green wanted to go back home. But his mother was convinced Louisville was a better opportunity than the segregated deep South.

"I look at what happened at the bus station as a test," said Green. "If I had quit, just climbed back on a bus and gone home . . . I wonder if I ever would have made it to the NFL."

* * *

Green became a star at Louisville and he entered the 1962 NFL draft. But the experience was much like his high school recruiting. He had graduated from Louisville with honors with a business degree. He had excelled on the football field. (You will find several stories saying he rushed for about 1,586 yards in his college career, but not a lot of other information is available.) But there was little attention from coaches at the next level.

"NFL teams would send out letters wanting to know your height, weight and time in the 40-yard dash," said Green. "I never had anyone from the NFL talk to me. I suppose they talked to (Louisville coach) Frank Camp, but I don't know for sure."

The NFL wasn't a small world in 1962, it was a village. Teams had few (if any) full-time scouts. Most head coaches also served as general managers. As for those forms, Green joked you could write down anything about your size and 40-yard time. Who was checking? After the top 25 to 50 players, scouting was mostly word of mouth: A scout knew a coach who saw a kid who "looked pretty good" . . .

Green was scouted in person as a third baseman, which he also played at Louisville. The Detroit Tigers offered him a chance to start a career in the minors. But he wanted to play football, where there would be no trip to the minors.

"I knew the NFL draft was happening and I thought I'd be

picked," said Green. "But there was no way to follow it. I don't think teams even had a phone number for me."

* * *

The big name in the 1962 draft was Ernie Davis, a running back from Jim Brown's alma mater, Syracuse University.

Davis was the first African-American to win the Heisman Trophy. He was the No. 1 pick in the 1962 draft by Washington. Browns coach Paul Brown was so enthralled with the idea of teaming Davis and Jim Brown in the Cleveland backfield, he traded future Hall of Famer Bobby Mitchell to Washington for the Syracuse star. Davis then signed the richest rookie contract in NFL history, $65,000 over three years.

But Davis was diagnosed with leukemia before playing a regular-season NFL game. He died on May 18, 1963.

Meanwhile, it was a member of the Louisville coaching staff who let Green know he was drafted—by the Green Bay Packers. While Ernie Davis was the top pick in 1962, Ernie Green was the last pick in the 14th round—196th overall.

"I eventually talked to Coach (Vince) Lombardi, and then one of his assistants," said Green. "They told me about being picked in the 14th round. They told me when training camp opened."

His contract was a $1,500 bonus, a salary (not guaranteed) of $8,500 and a chance to go to Green Bay. When he joined the Packers, the backfield was crowded, starting with future Hall of Famers Jim Taylor and Paul Hornung. They also picked running back Earl Gros in the first round (No. 14) in the same draft as Green. Add in solid veteran Elijah Pitts, and there was no room left.

"This was back when an NFL team would play a team of college all-stars in Chicago," said Green. "We were going by bus and the rookies were on the same bus with the coaches."

"I have a rookie who can help you," Vince Lombardi told Paul Brown. "The kid's name is Ernie Green. . . . He isn't going to make our team, but he's good enough to play in the league." He sure was. *Cleveland Press Collection, Cleveland State University Archives*

As Green got on the bus, he heard Lombardi tell an assistant coach, "It's a shame that kid will never get to play again."

Later on, Green realized Lombardi was talking about Ernie Davis.

* * *

Most fans don't know that Lombardi worshiped Paul Brown, whom he credited with helping him become the Packers' head coach. Early in Lombardi's career, he received a call from Brown. The veteran coach had a couple of defensive players who weren't going to make the Cleveland roster. Brown said, "They'll help you."

Their names were Henry Jordan and Willie Davis, and they became Hall of Fame defensive linemen.

In 1962, Lombardi was going to return the favor.

According to legendary Plain Dealer sports writer Chuck Heaton, "Vince called Paul at Hiram College one August afternoon. 'I have a rookie who can help you,' he said. 'The kid's name is Ernie Green. . . . He isn't going to make our team, but he's good enough to play in the league.' "

In a 1964 story, Heaton characterized Paul Brown as "being desperate for a running back. . . . Paul said, 'Send him along.' "

Green came to the Browns for a future seventh-round pick.

There is another part of the story. Paul Brown knew nothing about Green, other than he'd played at Louisville. But Brown's top assistant was Blanton Collier, who had coached at Kentucky. Collier called Louisville coach Frank Camp, who gave Green a strong endorsement.

The deal was made.

Meanwhile, the Packers were playing a preseason game in Dallas. Green received word to go to Lombardi's hotel room.

"I kept thinking they were sending me home," said Green.

Green knew he looked "shaky" as he met the coach.

"Take it easy," said Lombardi. "I'm not cutting you. Sit down."

Green sat and waited.

"This is a numbers game," said Lombardi. "I'm going to trade you to Cleveland. Paul Brown and I are very good friends. In fact, Paul talked me into taking this job."

With that, Green went to Cleveland. When he arrived, Paul Brown said, "Welcome to the Browns. We understand you can play. Get yourself together and get ready to play."

Green waited for more.

"But that was all he said," recalled Green.

Nothing was guaranteed for Green. Brown would post a list on the bulletin board.

"If your name wasn't on the list or a coach didn't get you, then you were OK," said Green. "No news was good news."

But Green's heart raced and his throat became dry a few times while checking that list before he finally made the team.

He didn't play much as a rookie, the Browns going with Charlie Scales and Tommy Wilson next to Jim Brown. Cleveland was 7-6-1 that season. When it was over, owner Art Modell fired Paul Brown.

Collier became the new coach and that was a huge break for Green. Collier was an Ernie Green fan, and Green would now be taking over next to Jim Brown.

"I was there to block and catch the football," said Green. "My skills were complementary to Jim's. The few times I ran the ball, I ran it pretty well."

Green averaged 4.8 yards per carry during his seven-year career.

"That sweep we ran so much," said Green. "If I didn't block the defensive end or the linebacker, it would be blown up right away. I got a big kick out of doing those kinds of things. . . . If you look up Jim's or Leroy Kelly's history, I was in the backfield with both of them. I believe in my heart I played a key role in helping them get to the Hall of Fame because that was my job."

* * *

You can win some bets with this trivia question: Who led the title winning 1964 Browns in touchdowns?

Most fans will guess Jim Brown. Or perhaps, receivers Gary Collins and Paul Warfield.

Since this chapter is about Ernie Green, you know the answer.

"It wasn't easy being Ernie Green," Paul Warfield once told me.

"He could run the football. He could catch the football. He had the total game. But he had to put his ego aside to block for Jim Brown."

Green's greatest gifts were speed, agility and intelligence. Blocking was not playing to his strength, but it was his main job. Even after Brown retired following the 1965 season, Green still had to block for Leroy Kelly. The Browns were loaded with gifted running backs during this era.

Brown rarely mentioned Green. He took time to praise his offensive line for their blocking.

"To Jim, I was a 14th round draft choice who grew up in Georgia and went to a small college," said Green. "That's it. We didn't talk a lot."

Warfield said there were times when Green had to look up to the heavens and ask, "Why me? Why did I have to end up on the same team as Jim Brown?"

Warfield and others on that team said Green never complained about being ignored by the public and media when playing next to Brown. When I wrote "Browns Town 1964," Green was perhaps the player on that team most respected by his teammates—because no one sacrificed more of his game for the good of the Browns. The consensus was Green could have been a featured back and a 1,000-yard rusher on many other teams.

He averaged 4.8 yards per carry for his career. He made two Pro Bowls despite being overshadowed by Jim Brown and Leroy Kelly.

In 1966, Green was given his biggest role in the offense. Jim Brown had retired, and the Browns were only just learning about the greatness of Kelly, who had been a backup to Green and Brown in 1964 and 1965.

That season, Green rushed for 750 yards (5.2-yard average) and caught 45 passes. He scored nine touchdowns. But Kelly cut loose for 1,141 yards (5.5 average) and scored 16 touchdowns in his first season as a starter.

It was a little like teaming with Jim Brown all over again for Green.

"Even though Leroy was our primary runner, I felt more a part of the offense after Jim left," said Green. "Leroy was my roommate. We were very close."

A knee injury cut Ernie Green's career short at the age of 30. He formed Ernie Green Industries (EGI) in Dayton. It eventually grew to a company making wheel coverings and other devices. He splits time between Dayton and Florida.

"To this day, I still have my season tickets," he said. "I loved playing for the Browns. The fans are super. I still receive mail 3-4 times a week from Browns fans. The Browns are like one of my children, I love them no matter what."

THIS BROWNS PLAYER CHANGED MY LIFE

I've been writing about sports for nearly five decades. In that span, I've talked to thousands of players, coaches and front office people. Only one changed my life. That was Bill Glass, a Pro Bowl defensive end for the Browns in the 1960s.

While I'm old, I'm not old enough to have covered Glass as a player. I met him in 1997, when I was writing "Browns Town 1964." In some ways, that book was patterned after Roger Kahn's "The Boys Of Summer." Kahn was a young baseball writer in New York covering the Brooklyn Dodgers in the 1950s. The book talked about that experience. But the section that intrigued me most was what happened to the players after their baseball careers ended.

That was what I wanted to cover with "Browns Town 1964." It began with the firing of Paul Brown after the 1962 season and told the story of the Browns winning the 1964 NFL title. But it also told stories about what became of several members of that championship team.

Many of those men did exceptional things after football. But none quite matched that of Bill Glass.

"I was going to the seminary while playing football," said Glass. "Because I was an athlete who was very public about his faith, I was already speaking at some churches and places like that."

Glass was 6-foot-5 and listed at 255 pounds in his playing days. Now, that sounds normal—even a bit thin—for a defensive end. In the 1960s, Glass was huge.

Then there was his position. Pass rusher. Tackler. Quarterback Cruncher.

"I remember seeing Bill deck this quarterback," said Tom Melody, a former Akron Beacon Journal sportswriter. "Bill really hit the guy. Later, Bill told me he thought he nearly killed the guy."

OK, nothing special about that story.

"There's more," said Melody. "After knocking down the quarterback, Bill also hit the ground. Then Bill looked at the quarterback, and he was worried. Bill then crawled on his hands and knees to see if the guy was OK. He didn't do one of those sack dances over the guy like they do today."

Heading into the 2021 season, Glass still had the team's single-season sack record with 16.5 in 1965.

"Bill wasn't a man's man as it was defined by pro football back then," former Browns defensive end Paul Wiggin told me.

Glass didn't swear. He didn't drink. He didn't chase women on the road. But on the field, he was a force.

"He wasn't a mean guy," said Wiggin. "But he'd take shots. He'd hit the quarterback hard. Then he'd kind of stay there, maybe help the guy up and pat him on the butt."

Glass would be celebrated more as a player today than in his day. Pass rushers are loved by the modern NFL, analytics valuing them right after quarterbacks in terms of what they should be paid.

Glass never thought much about that. Rather, he wanted to be part of a winning team, a good teammate and also to show a Christian could succeed in the brutal business of the NFL.

"Christianity is not being a non-competitive pushover," said Glass. "I was in a profession where my job was to rush the quarterback and be a tough guy. If I went out there and was a patsy, that's not a good influence for my cause. I had to be the best I could be."

But what about the inherent violence in the game?

"I didn't do anything dirty," said Glass. "I was never once penalized for excessive roughness. If I hit a quarterback late, it was an accident. I'd throw up my hands. I'd apologize to him. I didn't pick up quarterbacks and grind them into the dirt like some people do today."

When Glass spoke at churches and to Christian groups, he would be asked about his faith at work in the NFL. He knew people were watching him. He had to be effective. But he also had to "play within the lines," his view of the way the game should be played.

Glass is a member of the College Football Hall of Fame, having played at Baylor. He was a first-round draft choice by the Detroit Lions in 1957 and was later traded to Cleveland. His career lasted 11 seasons. He made four Pro Bowls.

"When we won the (1964) title, I was making $25,000," said Glass. "We got a bonus of $8,000 for beating the Colts. I also had some incentives in my contract for making the Pro Bowl and other things—that led to $6,000 in bonuses."

Add it all up, Glass said he made slightly less than $40,000 that 1964 season. He believes he was the highest paid defensive lineman in the NFL at that time.

He took the $8,000 bonus and bought a ranch in rural Texas covering 1,172 acres.

"I sold it about 10 years later, then used that money to buy some land near Dallas," he said.

That land was located in what is now known as Arlington, which is between Dallas and Fort Worth. He then sold that land for a profit.

Bill Glass still has the team's single-season sack record with 16.5 in 1965.
Cleveland Press Collection, Cleveland State University Archives

While Glass had a solid financial foundation, he was also "building up treasures in heaven," as the Bible says.

* * *

"After I retired, I wanted to be the next Billy Graham," said Glass.

Glass had spoken at a few rallies held by the man who was considered America's greatest evangelist during that era.

"I saw myself speaking in big stadiums to giant crowds," said Glass. "I thought I'd speak at city-wide rallies. In college, I knew I was called to ministry, but never saw myself as a regular pastor. I sensed it would be something different."

Different, indeed.

And he did become "the next Billy Graham," only it was the Billy Graham of the prison system. Prison ministry is more common now. Many were inspired by Bill Glass, who was a pioneer in the field. The most notable is Prison Fellowship, started by former Watergate figure Chuck Colson.

Glass retired from football after the 1968 season. He was speaking at churches and some city-wide ministries.

In Akron, he knew a Christian banker named Gordon Heffern who was involved in helping prisoners find jobs when they were released.

"He found thousands of them jobs over the years," said Glass. "But so many of them went back to prison. Gordon said we needed more than jobs, we needed to change their hearts."

Heffern challenged Glass to "do a city-wide event" behind the walls of a prison. Heffern said get some former athletes and others to go with Glass to speak to the prisoners.

Glass had no interest in doing that. He still had his eyes on the big public ministries. Prison was a foreign culture to him. No one in his family had been imprisoned.

"If you have any guts, you'll try prison," said Heffern. "If you believe Christ is the answer to change a person's life, you'll go where it's really tough. In fact, you're a wimp if you don't try prison. Even if it doesn't work out, the experience will be healthy for you."

This went on for a few years. Heffern was on the board of Bill Glass Ministries. He'd bring it up, challenging Glass to go where very few ministers (other than ministers employed by the prison system) were willing to venture.

Then, four years after he retired from the Browns, Glass

relented. Heffern set up a meeting with Pete Perini, who played for the Browns in 1955. At this point, Perini was warden of Marion Correctional Institution in central Ohio. As Glass and Perini talked, Glass knew he had to "do this right," he said. He couldn't show up, talk for a few hours, sign some autographs and leave.

Perini agreed to let Glass and his crew have complete access to the prison for an entire weekend.

"We'll eat meals with the inmates," said Glass. "I'll recruit 50 counselors and they need time to talk to the inmates, 1-on-1. They'll pay their own expenses, but they need access to the prison yard."

As Glass talked to Perini, he was creating a vision of a Billy Graham-type rally behind bars.

Just as a lot of people wouldn't go to church to hear Graham but would go to a stadium or another "non-Christian" venue, Glass thought the same would be true in prison. Glass didn't want to speak in the prison chapel. Do it in the gym. Do it in the yard. Do it on the baseball field, which became the center of the ministry at Marion.

He had former players talk about football. He had a juggler and other acts. He wanted to bring relief to the inmates. Then they'd talk about faith. But the real work was done with the volunteers, who would talk to inmates during informal settings.

The hulking Glass, who limped a bit from his days with the Browns, certainly "didn't seem like a church guy."

Perini loved the weekend. He contacted other wardens. Soon, Glass was hearing from prisons across the country asking him to come put on weekend programs.

He didn't find prison ministry, it found him.

And Glass found a message that spoke to the inmates: the lack of an earthly father in their lives. He was one of the first to recognize what is now called "the father problem" in society.

* * *

I didn't go to prison with Glass when I wrote about him for "Browns Town 1964." But a year later, I was in Chicago covering the Cleveland Indians during a big series against the White Sox. I heard from Ron Kuntz, who was a sports photographer from United Press International out of Cleveland. He and I were casual friends.

"Hey Terry, I'm with Bill Glass in Chicago," he said. "We're at Cook County Jail. Why don't you join us for the afternoon before tonight's game? I'll pick you up. It can make a good story for you."

I had been intrigued by Glass and his work when talking to him for "Browns Town 1964." I had never been inside a prison or a jail. A story on a former Brown as the Billy Graham of the prison system would have wide appeal.

At this point, my own faith was growing. I knew God wanted me to do something, but I was not sure what.

I followed Glass around Cook County Jail, an aging, dark, stinking facility. Glass had me walk around the prison yard with some of the volunteers. Soon, I was talking to some inmates.

I heard some very sad stories. A few guys even cried when talking about how they "messed up" (only not using those words). Glass had given his talk about the lack of fathers and the toll it takes on people—and how God can be a heavenly father.

That opened up lots of areas of conversation with guys on a 1-on-1 basis. By the end of the day, I ended up praying with a few of them. My journalistic walls went down.

* * *

I wrote a story about that afternoon in Chicago with Bill Glass for the Akron Beacon Journal. That led to a call from a minister at Summit County Jail for me to be involved in a day when they handed out shoe boxes of gifts to inmates for Christmas.

Bill Glass wanted to be the next Billy Graham, until a friend told him, "If you have any guts, you'll try prison."
Jim Gayle / The Plain Dealer

Would that make a good story? I went and wrote it. My friend Lee Owens (then football coach at the University of Akron) came along. He brought some players. One of them found his brother behind bars, his brother who had disappeared years ago.

Harry Watson was the chaplain at the Summit County Jail. He asked me to come back and speak at one of the services. I was nervous, but did so. Then I realized God was calling me to this ministry.

Like Bill Glass, I had no prison background. But dealing with athletes in different circumstances was good training.

I then went on at least a dozen prison weekends with Glass. In the meantime, I was being asked to do more local ministry. I knew being with Glass would be good training.

It's hard to know why God calls us to do certain things. But they usually are well out of our comfort zones.

Prison/jail ministry is not for most people. The conditions are primitive. The inmates tend to be respectful, because the services are voluntary. If they were required, it would be a different story.

But that was late in 1998 when the jail doors swung open. By 2000, I was doing weekly jail ministry and building my own small team with my wife Roberta, my friends Gloria Williams, Steve Haley and Frank Williams.

Our team has stayed together ever since.

And it started with the story of the 1964 Browns. Then a call from Ron Kuntz, and another story. Then a call from the Summit County Jail.

Like Glass, it's something I never envisioned for my life. But soon, it became a very big part of how I live.

ACKNOWLEDGMENTS

I would like to thank Bernie Kosar, Ozzie Newsome and so many other Browns players who were interviewed for this book and my series of stories in The Plain Dealer.

Former Browns GM Ernie Accorsi and public relations director Kevin Byrne were especially helpful.

Larry Pantages is the Bernie Kosar of researchers and editors. My wife Roberta transcribed interviews and did the first read and edit on the manuscript. This is book No. 32 and she has been there for all of them.

John Luttermoser is my top draft pick for copy editor.

From the Plain Dealer/Cleveland.com, David Campbell and Chris Quinn have been extremely supportive in my writing.

Faith Hamlin has been my wonderful agent since the Bernie Kosar era.

Finally, David Gray has been my publisher since 2000. No one does it better.

OTHER BOOKS BY TERRY PLUTO . . .

Browns Town 1964

The Cleveland Browns and the 1964 Championship

Terry Pluto

A nostalgic look back at the upstart AFC Cleveland Browns' surprising 1964 championship victory over the hugely favored Baltimore Colts. Profiles the colorful players who made that season memorable, including Jim Brown, Paul Warfield, Frank Ryan. Recreates an era and a team for which pride was not just a slogan.

"Pluto movingly reveals the substance of a mythic bond between men and a game, a team and a city—and thus lays bare how present-day pro football has surrendered its soul." – Kirkus Reviews

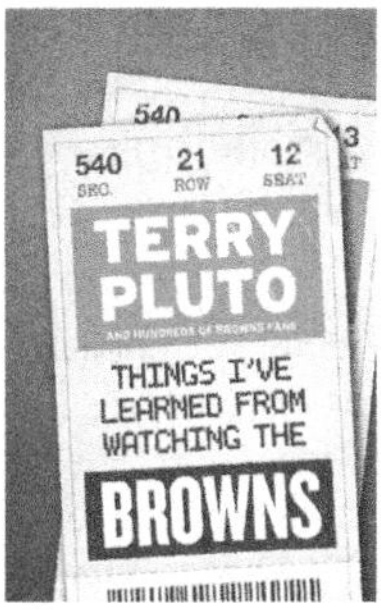

Things I've Learned from Watching the Browns

Terry Pluto

Veteran sports writer Terry Pluto asks Cleveland Browns fans: Why, after four decades of heartbreak, teasing, and futility, do you still stick with this team? Their stories, coupled with Pluto's own insight and analysis, deliver the answers. Like any intense relationship, it's complicated. But these fans just won't give up.

"For dedicated Browns fans [the book is] like leafing through an old family photo album." – BlogCritics.com

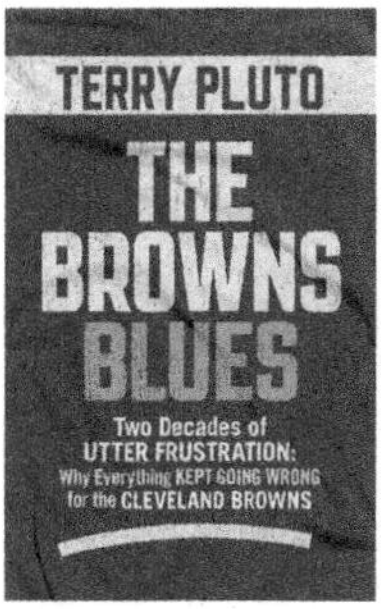

The Browns Blues

Two Decades of Utter Frustration: Why Everything Kept Going Wrong for the Cleveland Browns

Terry Pluto

How could things go so wrong for so long? From their return in 1999 through the winless 2017 season, the Cleveland Browns had the worst record in the NFL. And their fans had ulcers. Veteran sports columnist Terry Pluto explains two decades of front-office upheaval and frustrating football in this detailed, behind-the-scenes analysis.

OTHER BOOKS BY TERRY PLUTO . . .

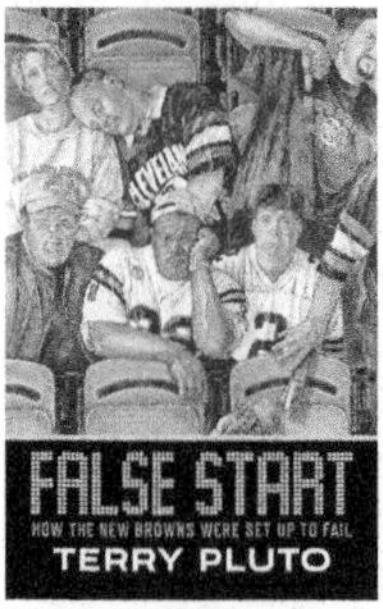

False Start

How the New Browns Were Set Up to Fail

Terry Pluto

A hard look at the unhappy beginnings of the post-1999 Cleveland Browns franchise, this book chronicles the backroom deals, big-money power plays, poor decisions, and plain bad luck that dogged the venerable franchise after Art Modell skipped town in 1995. How long should fans have to wait for a winner? A book the NFL does not want you to read.

"[A book] NFL fans in general and Browns' fans in particular will definitely want to read . . . a fascinating, behind-the-scenes look at how the new Browns were created and what's kept them from making the progress everyone expected." – Houston Chronicle

Glory Days in Tribe Town

The Cleveland Indians and Jacobs Field 1994–1997

Terry Pluto, Tom Hamilton

Relive the most thrilling seasons of Indians baseball in recent memory! Cleveland's top sportswriter teams up with the Tribe's veteran radio announcer and fans to share favorite stories from the first years of Jacobs Field, when a star-studded roster (Belle, Thome, Vizquel, Ramirez, Alomar, Nagy) and a sparkling ballpark captivated an entire city.

Our Tribe

A Baseball Memoir

Terry Pluto

A son, a father, a baseball team. Sportswriter Terry Pluto's memoir tells about growing up and learning to understand a difficult father through their shared love of an often awful baseball team. Baseball can be an important bridge across generations, sometimes the only common ground. This story celebrates the connection.

"A beautiful, absolutely unforgettable memoir." – Booklist

More at **www.grayco.com**

OTHER BOOKS BY TERRY PLUTO . . .

The Curse of Rocky Colavito

A Loving Look at a Thirty-Year Slump

Terry Pluto

A baseball classic. No sports fans suffered more miserable teams for more seasons than Indians fans of the 1960s, '70s, and '80s. Here's a fond and often humorous look back at "the bad old days" of the Tribe. The definitive book about the Indians of that generation, and a great piece of sports history writing.

"The year's funniest and most insightful baseball book." – Chicago Tribune

Vintage Cavs

A Warm Look Back at the Cavaliers of the Cleveland Arena and Richfield Coliseum Years

Terry Pluto

The Cleveland Arena and Richfield Coliseum are long gone, but they and the Cavaliers teams from 1970 to the 1990s come alive in this personal history by a sportswriter who was there as a young fan and later an NBA beat writer. From expansion team to the brink of greatness with Austin Carr, World B. Free, "Hot Rod" Williams, Mark Price, and others.

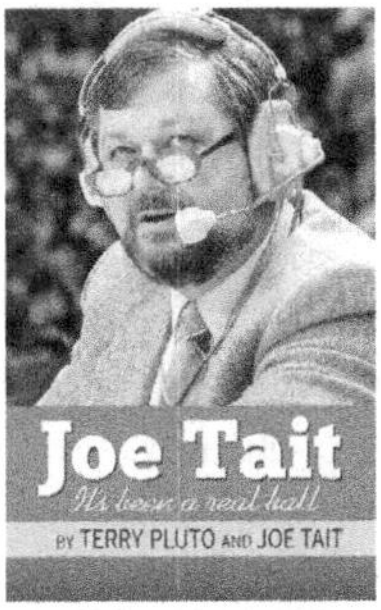

Joe Tait: It's Been a Real Ball

Stories from a Hall-of-Fame Sports Broadcasting Career

Terry Pluto, Joe Tait

Legendary broadcaster Joe Tait is like an old family friend to three generations of Cleveland sports fans. This book celebrates the inspiring career of "the Voice of the Cleveland Cavaliers" with stories from Joe and dozens of fans, colleagues, and players. Hits the highlights of a long career and also uncovers some touching personal details.

"An easy, fun book to read and will surely bring back good memories for Cleveland sports fans who listened to Tait's trademark calls since 1970." – 20SecondTimeout.com

More at **www.grayco.com**

OTHER BOOKS BY TERRY PLUTO . . .

The Comeback: LeBron, the Cavs & Cleveland

How LeBron James Came Home and Brought a Championship to Cleveland

Terry Pluto

One of the greatest Cleveland sports stories ever! In this epic homecoming tale, LeBron James and the Cavaliers take fans on a roller coaster ride from despair to hope and, finally, to glory as the 2016 NBA champions. Terry Pluto tells how it all happened, with insightful analysis and behind-the-scenes details.

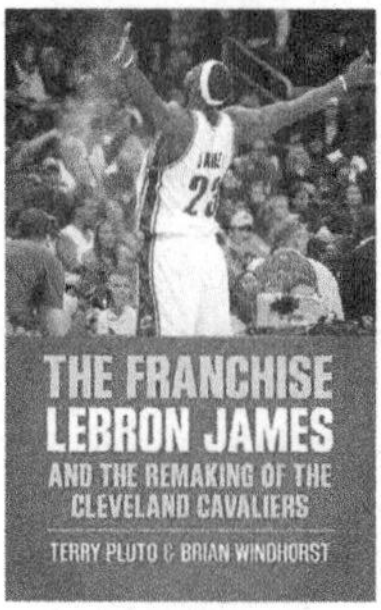

The Franchise

LeBron James and the Remaking of the Cleveland Cavaliers

Terry Pluto, Brian Windhorst

An in-depth look at how a team and a city were rebuilt around LeBron James. Two award-winning sports journalists tell the converging stories of a struggling franchise and a hometown teenage phenom. Will fascinate basketball fans who want the inside story of a young superstar shouldering the weight of an entire NBA franchise.

"Not your typical sports biography . . . Take[s] the reader behind the scenes in the Cavaliers' front office, revealing how championship contenders are built" – Library Journal

Faith and You Vol. 1

Essays on Faith in Everyday Life

Terry Pluto

Thoughtful essays on faith in everyday life from award-winning sportswriter Terry Pluto, who has also earned a reputation—and a growing audience—for his down-to-earth musings on spiritual subjects. Topics include choosing a church, lending money to friends, dealing with jerks, sharing your faith, visiting the sick, even planning a funeral.

More at **www.grayco.com**